D0394419

How to
Make Love
to a Man (safely)

How to
Make Love
to a Man (safely)

a new, intimate guide
to sexy sex
in the nineties

Alexandra Penney
with Susan Dooley

CAROL SOUTHERN BOOKS/NEW YORK

Published by Carol Southern Books, 201 East 50th Street, New
York, New York 10022. Member of the Crown Publishing Group.

Random House, Inc. New York, Toronto, London, Sydney,
Auckland

CAROL SOUTHERN BOOKS and colophon are trademarks of Crown
Publishers, Inc.

Manufactured in the United States of America

ISBN 0-517-59423-4

For American women

ACKNOWLEDGMENTS

Many people have helped to create this book:
Susie Dooley is the paragon collaborator, and Carol
Southern the ultimate editor. I am deeply grateful for
their help. Ed Victor, agent extraordinare, is a guiding
spirit (as well as good for a lot of laughs).

Immense thank-yous and a special citation to Joe
Amodio and Catherine Heusel. You can't find two better, faster, smarter researchers anywhere in the world.

Grateful thanks to the following friends and colleagues who, for democratic purposes, are listed in al-
phabetical order: Larry Burstein (*Self's* super-
publisher), Deborah Cavanaugh, Erin Dracos, Judy
Kent (my right hand), Mary Maguire, Barbara Marks,
Dr. Allen Mead, Andy Plesser (my devoted p.r. man),
James Santier (who kept me in great shape), Maggie
Scarf, Paul Scherer, Deborah Sharpe, Michelle Si-
drane, Dr. Frank Silverman, Peter and Ellen Straus,
Larry Totah, Dr. John B. Train, Rochelle Udell (fabulous art director), Nicholas von Hoffman (who pro-
vided a daily pep-talk), X (the man who is worried
about spilled pea soup), and, of course, the elusive
and incomparable Tuna B. Fish, who is, as ever, the
delight of my life.

I am forever indebted to the genius boss-man at
Condé Nast, Si Newhouse, and to every person on the
sensational *Self* staff.

Lastly, I want to acknowledge the profound influ-
ence of the founding editor of *Self*, the woman who
was responsible for the first *How to Make Love to a
Man*, Phyllis Starr Wilson.

Contents

Part One · Being Safe

Part Two · Being Sexy

Resources

Part One
Being Safe

one

Lean, Lithe, and Gorgeous

He's dark, intense, romantic, incredibly sexy, and he's fallen deeply in love with her. She's blond, has no idea how beautiful she is, and she can't believe he's really interested in her. They've been playing cat and mouse since they met at work a few weeks earlier. Finally they've been on their first date, and afterward they go back to her place.

Minutes later he's taking her into his arms, softly kissing her hair, her eyes, her lips, and leading her by the hand to the bed in her small studio apartment. His kisses are warm and searching and she finally lets herself go, lying on the bed, kicking off her shoes, unbuttoning her dress, kissing him back with all the passion he had been so certain was in her.

"You have something?" she asks.

"You mean rubbers?" he says, stopping a kiss. "Talk about a mood changer."

"Well, do you?"

He doesn't.

She gets up and sits on the side of the bed.

"What would that have looked like?" he asks. "It would've looked like I was planning to do it with you."

She tells him it's okay, perhaps this scenario was not such a good idea anyway.

She gets up, straightens her dress, goes to the kitchenette, and pulls out some leftover meatloaf to slice up for sandwiches. "Oh!" She's cut her finger and he quickly heads to the bathroom to find a Band-Aid. She repeats her doubts about him. "I'm a BLT sort of person," she says. "And I think you're looking for someone a little more pheasant under glass."

Not responding, he locates a Band-Aid in the medicine chest, and, after carefully, tenderly cleaning her wound, wraps it around her finger. The atmosphere lightens as he confesses that he's older than he said he was. She admits fibbing about her age, too.

They hesitantly begin to kiss again.

She turns toward the living room, calling out, ". . . in the medicine cabinet. I didn't want you to get the wrong impression." He retrieves the condoms and, grinning, walks back to the bed, where she's flung off her dress and nestled under the covers. She's holding out her arms to him and smiling . . .

Frankie and Johnny, which stars Al Pacino and Michelle Pfeiffer, and in which this dialogue by Terrence McNally occurs, was the first film I saw where a man and woman faced the reality of Nineties sex—sex with condoms. As I sat there in the darkened theater, I realized that the two stars were acting out the dilemma most couples face today. There is no longer room in the world for thoughtless passion or the kind of irresponsible sex that "just happens."

The same week that I watched Pacino and Pfeiffer sparring and loving, I heard the news about Magic Johnson and how he had contracted AIDS through heterosexual sex. It was no longer something that happened to "others"—to homosexuals, or drug addicts, or people who had been given transfusions of infected blood. It could happen to any of us.

Ten years ago I wrote *How to Make Love to a Man* because nothing had been written on what men wanted physically and emotionally when it came to sex. Today, it's clear that unless you're in a long-term monogamous relationship, making love to a man is going to involve several new elements: the condom and nonoxynol-9, and getting to know each other before going to bed.

I decided to write *How to Make Love to a Man (Safely)* for three reasons. The first is because I haven't seen a book or an article that gives all the facts about sex in the age of AIDS and sexually transmitted diseases without sounding like a physician's clinical take-home pamphlet.

Sex, I devoutly believe, is still—and will always be—sexy. Avoiding casual sex and using a condom properly should by no means take the pleasure out of one of the most gratifying activities known to humankind. I felt that a book that gave all the facts about safe, healthy sex could be a sexy book that was encouraging and helpful instead of making us fearful and uncomfortable.

The second reason that I wanted to write this book is that I wanted to report on some very exciting sex research. NEMOs, U spot orgasms, the CAT position—these are some of the new and fascinating areas on making love that this book will cover.

Third, as editor of *Self* magazine for almost four years, I have been involved on a day-to-day basis with women's health concerns. Healthy sex is one of these issues and I believe that the information you'll be reading here can help to save women's—and men's—lives.

My friend and colleague Susan Dooley, a journalist and researcher who formerly wrote a column for the *Washington Post*, helped me with the research and writing of *How to Make Love to a Man (Safely)*. Between us we interviewed over a hundred single and married men aged twenty to seventy-two. This is neither a sociological tract nor a scientific treatise but a practical guide with input from men from all parts of the country who represent all different economic, ethnic, and educational backgrounds.

We wanted to know what men think about sexual relationships now that we live under the cloud of AIDS. We wanted to know about condoms and lubricants, which ones are the best, how best to use them, how men prefer a woman to bring up the subject, if they want a woman to buy condoms and have them available, and what experiences men have had with safe, healthy sex that they thought might be valuable for women to know.

We also asked lots of other questions: what is sexy in a woman today, have women become more skillful in making love to a man over the past ten years, how many men have experienced multiple or non-ejaculatory orgasms, what is the best sex they ever had, how do they like to be touched, whether oral sex is still so important to them and how best to do it.

We also talked to dozens of women about their experiences with safe sex, and we interviewed gynecologists, general practitioners, therapists, sex researchers, psychologists, and sociologists on the subject.

Sex is about pleasure, but it is also about health. Long before AIDS, sexually active humans faced the fatal scourges of syphilis and gonorrhea. It is only recently we have enjoyed sex as a no-risk entertainment, courtesy of antibiotics, abortion, and the Pill. In addition, all the focus on AIDS is causing us to forget that there are plenty of other sexually transmitted diseases out there. Not only are these diseases dangerous in and of themselves, they are associated with an increased risk for AIDS.

I've tried to use a commonsense approach to analyzing the mass of clinical information on sex and health and to clarify it for myself, and for you, the reader. Whether you're single, married, divorced, or living with a lover, you'll see how AIDS does and does not affect you, your man, and your family.

The first part of this book is about *being safe*. I'll cover the latest facts about HIV (the virus that causes AIDS) who's at risk and why, and the most recent information about AIDS tests. You'll read about how to bring up the issue of condoms with your man, including some easy conversation-starters, then you'll learn the art of condom connoisseurship and how to use a condom when you're making love.

The second part of the book is on *being sexy*. You'll also learn about the exciting news in making love, you'll gain some interesting insights into the male psyche, and you'll find out what's the latest in sex research—it's really fascinating stuff. I think that you'll want to try at least some of the new, provocative erotic techniques outlined in these pages.

Lastly, one of the most important points I want to make in *How to Make Love to a Man (Safely)* is that I believe that out of every crisis an opportunity arises. The horror and fear of AIDS has made it necessary for us to get to know one another before we become physically intimate and to speak honestly and openly about our innermost feelings. This communication can only lead to a better understanding of each other and, eventually, to the kind of deep, long-lasting intimacy that many of us were searching for in the Eighties.

two

The Facts, Ma'am

When you write a book such as this one, you get very nosey and very personal very fast. Recently I stopped at my friend Marian's apartment for coffee. There was a note on the kitchen counter from her nineteen-year-old daughter: "Mom, please wake me when John calls."

"Is John the boyfriend?" I asked.

"For the moment," Marian sighed. "Carrie falls in love every few months."

"Aren't you worried about her? Do you know if

Carrie makes her boyfriends use condoms?" I wanted to know.

"No," Marian said. "She's been on the Pill since she was fifteen. I told her I was not in favor of sex at her early age, but that I would rather know she was prepared than discover that I was going to become a grandmother."

"No, I meant because of AIDS."

"Of course I've talked to her about AIDS. I told her she had to be careful, but these boys aren't street kids. For God's sake, we're talking about Stanford.

"We've been talking about AIDS," Marian informed her daughter, who had just come into the kitchen.

"And . . . ?" said Carrie with all the enthusiasm of a nineteen-year-old who's been out until three in the morning.

"I told her that you're careful. You are, aren't you?"

"Sure, Mom. Everyone makes a joke about it, 'Don't go out unless you wear your rubber,' but no one wants to get sick. I'm careful."

Marian looked pleased, but I wondered what being careful meant to Carrie.

"Do you always use condoms?" I asked.

"Most of the kids do," she replied. "I mean, kids may fool around without one on, but when it comes to actually doing it—you know—then they stop and put one on."

"Do you use ones with a nonoxynol-9 lubricant?"

She looked blankly at me. Although Carrie deserved good marks for trying to prevent pregnancy, she was not wise in the ways of HIV. Carrie and her friends seemed unaware that a condom, to be most effective in preventing disease transmission, must be used with a spermicide containing nonoxynol-9. Carrie also didn't know that it isn't enough to have a man withdraw and put on a condom just before he ejaculates. The condom must be in place before a man enters a woman or before oral sex takes place.

Another story: One man I interviewed said that many of the women he dated had never asked him to use a condom: "They assume I'm sufficiently prudent and middle-class not to have indulged in anything dangerous."

Did he use one anyway? "No." He sounded embarrassed. "I guess I assume the same about them."

Jack, a thirty-six-year-old real-estate broker from Miami, found out that such assumptions can be a mistake. "Joan was separated when I met her," he told me. "She was a friend of my sister's and we had an affair. I *knew* who she was, knew the kind of people she knew. We were from the same background. When we went to bed together, I did think about AIDS, but I didn't say anything, and I didn't use a condom because we'd talked about our pasts. She'd only been to bed with three men in her entire life—her husband and two guys she went out with after they split up.

"Last year she called me, hysterical. One of the guys

she'd gone out with? He was AC/DC. Someone had
seen him in a gay bar with his boyfriend. Joan was really freaked. So was I. We decided we'd both get
tested. It turned out to be okay, but it taught me
about trust. When I trusted Joan, I was also trusting
some guy I'd never met. And even if he hadn't been
bisexual, he might have been trusting some woman
who used drugs. AIDS spreads through too wide a circle. Forget trust. Now, before I go to bed with anyone, I tell her that story. I tell her that's why I use a
condom. And if I start seeing someone exclusively,
we'll wait six months and get tested. Trust *and* the
test. That's my motto now."

"Yes, I'm using condoms," said a divorced New
Yorker in his mid-forties. "But I don't want to spend
my life wearing them. I've started seriously looking
for a woman I can have a long-term relationship with.
I let a sexual relationship develop more slowly because, in the past, it was easy to let sex take over too
soon. Sometimes sex turned out to be the only thing
you had in common. If AIDS has taught me nothing
else, it's that going to bed with someone is not a good
way to get to know them."

From my conversations with men, I've learned that
some used condoms, some did not, some used them
sometimes, and a great many are reluctant to use them
even when asked. Some women asked men to use one,
some asked men to withdraw and put one on before
ejaculation, others did not even broach the subject.
This is *not* a good state of affairs.

In 1986, Surgeon General C. Everett Koop called the condom the first line of defense in the battle against AIDS. One year later, Masters and Johnson and Kolodny published the results of a nationwide study of the effects of the AIDS virus. "To think that condom use is perfect," they write, "or even near perfect, in eliminating the risk of HIV transmission is foolishness of the highest order."

Their view is alarming and cannot be discounted. But sex is not going to disappear and, at present, we do have two weapons against the virus that each of us can deploy: prudent behavior (more about this in the next chapter), and nonoxynol-9 with a properly used condom.

At the start of the AIDS crisis in the early Eighties, condoms were selling at about two hundred million per year. By the end of the Eighties, with Koop consistently urging condom use, that number had jumped to some four hundred million.

Condom consciousness had arrived. Or had it?

You'd think by now the number of condoms sold annually would be out of sight. But in 1991, sales *fell* by 4 percent. Sales in 1992 are expected to increase by about 5 percent, which, industry experts say, would put them back at the record 1990 level. This increase has been attributed almost entirely to a single event: the announcement by Magic Johnson that he has the virus that causes AIDS.

Women, who were once expected to be the biggest buyers of condoms, make up only 15 to 20 percent of the market. The media continues to send out mixed messages. There is a virtual ban on condom advertising campaigns on television despite the fact that, according to a recent Roper poll, many Americans are in favor of such commercials.

In November of 1992, Fox Broadcasting scheduled two condom advertisements during a show featuring the rock-and-roll band U2. But those were the first televised ads since Fox broke ranks with other networks to run the first national condom commercial the year before. What this makes a woman think is that the condom, despite its availability in rainbow colors, is still not nice.

Forget words like *nice* or *not nice*. To be healthy in the Nineties you must be aware of your behavior and learn to think of the condom as your life preserver. As an architect I spoke with put it: "Condoms are the seat belts of the Nineties."

The latest numbers on condom use tell an alarming story. In a study published in the journal *Science* (November 13, 1992), it was reported that of ten thousand Americans only 17 percent of those with multiple sex partners, 13 percent of those with a risky sexual partner, and 11 percent of those who had received blood transfusions before 1985 have adopted regular condom use.

Another survey is equally eye-opening: Of sixteen thousand women attending family-planning clinics in Pennsylvania, a whopping 72 percent of women who had casual sexual partners *never* used condoms.

To put it plainly: Men and women haven't gotten the condom message.

What Is AIDS? What Is HIV?

AIDS is frightening. And fear affects people in different ways. Some take a vow of celibacy, some retreat into total denial, some take "calculated risks." Some feel that AIDS will devour only promiscuous strangers; others believe that the virus is everywhere.

At a cocktail party not long ago, I overheard a woman say that 25 percent of the students in her suburban high school carried the AIDS virus. Short of testing every student—which hadn't been done—there is no way anyone could make that statement.

Ignore stuff like that. It's scare talk. It can scare the almost-monogamous Des Moines housewife into believing that her one brief affair fifteen years ago is going to reach out from the past and smite her dead. There is a lot that isn't known about AIDS, but there is a lot that is.

Human immunodeficiency virus (HIV) causes acquired immune deficiency syndrome (AIDS). AIDS is the end product of becoming infected with HIV—a virus that attacks certain cells of the immune system and eventually cripples the body's ability to fight off illness.

You can carry the AIDS virus (that is, HIV) and not have AIDS. At present it is believed that most people who carry the virus will develop AIDS, but some may not. Unfortunately, the notion that some may not is based more on hope than strong scientific data. There are so many unknowns to this illness that even the top scientists in the field can't answer many questions about how HIV leads to full-blown AIDS or if there are other paths that lead there as well. At the moment, asymptomatic HIV-positive patients are advised to avoid any other threats to their immune system and to do everything they can to bolster and protect their immune functioning through nutrition (a lot of work is being done with antioxidant enzymes), lifestyle changes, and sometimes medication.

According to the Centers for Disease Control and Prevention (CDC), which tracks AIDS data, it can take from eight to ten years from the time of infection for a person with HIV to develop full-blown AIDS. It is often difficult to tell just *when* a person was infected, so the time from *detection* to becoming ill is often much shorter.

Because new research can change medical opinion on what constitutes an unacceptable risk, I am including a resource list at the back of the book with phone numbers and sources you can contact to continue to keep up to date.

All the research indicates that where you live and, more important, how you live determines how likely you are to become infected. There are more reported AIDS cases in New York, which has the highest number in the nation, than in North Dakota, which has the lowest. There are more AIDS cases among people who indulge in certain risky practices than there are among those who do not.

Should you move from New York City to Bismarck to avoid AIDS?

No.

Should you change the way you behave?

Yes, and to do that, to protect yourself, you need to know how HIV is passed.

How the Virus Is Transmitted

The virus itself is surprisingly weak when outside the body. Something as simple as chlorine bleach kills HIV, as does the spermicide nonoxynol-9. When exposed to air, the virus quickly dies. So you cannot get HIV from clothes, phones, or toilet seats, or from everyday, nonintimate contact with an infected person.

Inside the body, however, HIV is tough and resourceful. It has been detected in almost every bodily fluid, including (in very small amounts) saliva, urine, tears, and breast milk. There is even evidence that the tiny virus (4 percent the size of a sperm) can be absorbed directly through mucous membranes that do not have any cuts or tears.

The CDC believes that HIV infection requires exposure to a large quantity of the virus and its *transmission therefore requires direct contact between an infected bodily fluid containing high amounts of the virus (like semen or blood) and the blood supply of an uninfected person.*

Therefore:

- If you or your sexual partner take drugs intravenously and share an infected needle and/or works, you are greatly at risk.
- If your partner has been sexually involved with a man who also has or has had sex with other men, you are greatly at risk.
- If you have multiple sexual partners, you are greatly at risk.
- If you practice unprotected anal sex with a partner who has not been tested, you are greatly at risk.
- If you or your partner had a blood transfusion before 1985, the year blood banks began screening donors for HIV, you are greatly at risk.

In general, the more partners you are involved with, the greater your risk, since multiple contacts not only increase your chance of encountering someone carrying the virus, they increase the risk of other sexually transmitted diseases. The genital sores that usually accompany such diseases make it easier for HIV to enter your body. Also, engaging in sex while intoxicated or on drugs impairs judgment—in both your choice of partners and your ability to use a condom properly.

While it is much easier for the virus to be transmitted from a man to a woman, uninfected men can contract the virus through infected vaginal fluids or menstrual blood.

TESTING

Since 1985, when the Food and Drug Administration (FDA) approved the first test for HIV, a flurry of other tests have come on the market. Today's tests are faster and safer for the clinician.

All testing methods will detect antibodies to the most common strain of HIV, HIV-1. However, HIV-2, an equally deadly strain that is prevalent among heterosexuals in West Africa, has begun showing up in Europe, Canada, and the United States. American blood centers have been screening for both strains of the virus since mid-1992. (To date, clinics and doctors are still only using the tests designed for HIV-1, which can detect HIV-2 in 60 to 90 percent of the cases. If you want to be tested specifically for HIV-2, ask your doctor. If your doctor cannot administer the test, he or she can refer you to someone who will.)

HIV tests are usually conducted in doctors' offices, clinics, and hospitals. The most recently approved test, the Murex SUDS HIV-1 Test, takes only ten minutes and can be processed in the doctor's office while you wait.

When performed in public clinics, the cost for AIDS tests is free; elsewhere, costs run from $5 to $150 depending on the tests. For an update on the tests now in use, see pages 141–143.

Whenever a person has been infected with HIV, it takes some time for antibodies to show up in the bloodstream. In most infected people, the antibodies can be detected approximately three months after in-fection. In some cases, however, they won't show up for six months or more. This means that if you en-gaged in risky sex in June, you need to wait until De-cember to take the test. *And during those six months, you cannot engage in any of the activities that put you at risk for AIDS without making the test results meaningless.*

The HIV test is simple. Coping with the results may not be, which is why all those who work with AIDS patients suggest that you call one of the AIDS hot lines (see pages 139–140) before you decide to take the test. The people who work on these phones are trained to answer questions about the confidentiality of the results, what questions you will be asked, and who in your area can provide help if you test positive.

In some areas of the country, you can be tested anonymously. The blood sample is labeled by num-ber, not by name, and no one but you will know the results. In other areas, you will have to settle for con-fidential testing, which means that, unless you sign a medical release, the results will be known only to you and to your doctor. However, you should know that in some areas if you apply for insurance, the test re-sults might be given out. The Centers for Disease Control's AIDS hot line can tell you if you live in an area where anonymous testing is possible and can counsel you on the consequences of testing positive.

Some people are afraid of taking the test. They see it as a death sentence. But remember that *the over-whelming odds are that you will test negative* and that if you *do* test positive, early diagnosis can help extend your life.

The Risk to Women

Even though many more men are HIV-positive than women (between 1981 and 1992, 248,000 American men had AIDS as opposed to 25,947 women), women are much more at risk from this disease than men because physiologically their bodies allow viruses more ease of entry. Few women are aware that, indeed, all sexually transmitted diseases are more easily transmitted from men to women than the reverse.

Women have always been in the majority among heterosexuals who are HIV-positive. Here's a statistical shocker: A 1991 study by researchers at the University of California, San Francisco, found that, if an HIV-negative woman practiced unsafe sex, the odds of her being infected by an HIV-positive partner were 17.5 to 1.

The CDC reports that between 1989 and 1990, the largest proportionate increases in AIDS cases were among women, African Americans, persons living in the South, and those exposed through heterosexual contact. Few of us seem to realize how endangered we are.

DO KISSES SPREAD AIDS?

Can we, at least, celebrate kissing? The answer is yes—
and a little bit no. Even though HIV has been found
in saliva, it's generally thought that the amount of
virus isn't enough to actually transmit the disease.
That doesn't mean there's absolutely no risk, though,
so you should take a few precautions. The best policy
to follow regarding kissing is to avoid it when you are
not sure of your partner and/or have canker sores,
bleeding gums, or open wounds in the mouth. Until
the sores heal, keep your mouth closed. And remember, love-bites, Dracula-style, are verboten.

HOW SAFE IS ORAL SEX?

If mouth to mouth might pass the virus but probably
won't, what about mouth to penis or vagina? Researchers have not found a high rate of transmission
of HIV through oral sex, though they do advise
women against swallowing the semen. (As you can
imagine, this is not a statistic that is easy to isolate.
The way cases are reported makes it very difficult to
know whether the infection has actually been passed
between people who have no other risk factors and
who engaged only in oral sex, instead of going on to
have full intercourse.) As with kissing, researchers are
unwilling to say transmission is impossible, just that it
is not as likely as it is in some other forms of sex.

To be entirely safe, don't give him oral sex unless

he is wearing a condom. Don't let him perform cunnilingus on you unless you lay a thin shield of latex over your vaginal area to keep his tongue from coming into direct contact with your genitals. Scientists hedge their bets on whether such protection is necessary or whether it is even effective. But if you're worried that you or your partner is at risk, use protective measures.

IS IT TRUE WHAT THEY SAY ABOUT ANAL SEX?

The riskiest sexual practice is unprotected anal sex. The blood vessels in the rectum are very close to the surface and easily torn, making transmission of the disease easier. *Never* have anal sex without using a condom unless you are absolutely certain that your partner is not carrying the HIV virus. This means having the HIV test and trusting in your partner's fidelity. Never let your lover move from the anus into the vagina without taking off and disposing of the old condom and putting on a fresh one.

ARE OTHER SEXUALLY TRANSMITTED DISEASES INVOLVED?

With all the media attention on AIDS, it's easy to forget that it was only a few years ago that *Time* magazine did a cover story on herpes. This contagious virus, which causes painful sores on genital areas, was spreading at a rate that made people decide free love might have a high price.

Herpes has been knocked offstage by the AIDS virus, but it is still a major health problem, infecting more than 20 million people in the United States and rising at the rate of half a million victims a year.

Other sexually transmitted diseases (STDs) on the rise are chlamydia (four million new cases a year!) and genital warts (one million cases a year). These diseases and others, like syphilis and gonorrhea (1.3 million new cases), play a part in the spread of AIDS.

When government health officials say they don't see AIDS spreading rapidly through heterosexual contact, they make an exception for people who have other sexually transmitted diseases. The genital sores that accompany many of these diseases can serve as an entrance for HIV. All of the STDs weaken the system, making it more susceptible to infection.

three

Love
Affairs
in the
Nineties

(Plus, The Art of Condom
Conversation)

In safe sex, as in everything to do with AIDS, how well you know your partner will dictate the cautions you take. Love, as always, is about trust. With AIDS, that trust should be based on the condom, the HIV test, and on long-term knowledge of the way a person behaves, not on a sudden affinity for big blue eyes. The days of being swept away by strangers in the night are finished and, as one woman said nostalgically, "the Golden Age of sex is over."

Adds a research editor I talked with, "Safe sex isn't strictly about love *or* trust. It's about biology. Viruses

don't have morals. . . . We have sense enough not to
cough or sneeze in our lovers' faces, but we don't
give potentially fatal viruses the same respect we give
the flu.''

So, hearing all this sobering news, how's a con-
temporary woman to maneuver sexually and still
have fun?

Carefully, that's how. Casual sex, sex with someone
you barely know, sex with multiple partners, these actions carry very real risks. "Sportfucking is an ancient
pastime now" is the way one man put it.

Picking up someone in a bar and taking him home
with you is just plain dumb. Allowing a man to seduce you before you feel comfortable and ready is a
no-no. Letting yourself lose control by having too
much to drink or taking drugs so that your normal ra-
tional self is not in operation can lead to dire consequences. It's a new age—and a new time.

This is not to say that we must return to the hypoc-
risy and strictures of the Fifties, when premarital sex
was frowned on and single women were considered
cheap if they had a lover.

Today's smart woman is concerned about her health
and also about healthy, sexy sex. Making love is still
one of the best things about being alive and you can
enjoy it as much as you ever did.

The reality is that AIDS and other STDs have made
alterations in our lives. But be aware that there's a
definite up side to this. Dating patterns have changed
to the benefit of both sexes. Men no longer have to

prove themselves with notches on their belts and they
don't need to boast about how fast they can get a
women to bed. Women no longer have to succumb to
the fear of losing someone they're interested in if they
don't sleep with them on the second or third date.
The sexual pressure is off in the Nineties.

But there is another kind of strain on all of us—
learning how to deal with the new sexual differences in
the age of AIDS, learning how to cope with, and talk
about, condoms, lubricants, tests, sexual histories, and
past lovers.

You're not alone if you're confused or feel ill at
ease with all this. Everyone I speak to feels the same.

Many of us hesitate to mention the condom early
enough because we're afraid we'll sound aggressive,
that we're assuming sex will be part of the picture,
that we might be thought of as promiscuous. But people who are in romantic situations where sex is a
likely event are finding imaginative ways to bring the
condom into conversation.

Angela, divorced and somewhere in her forties, lives
and teaches in Pittsburgh. Since her youngest daughter
left for school two years ago, Angela has felt freer to
enter the world of single sex.

"Great timing, right? Just when I'm about to go
have a good time, the good times are over."

As a teacher, Angela is very aware of AIDS. She has
given enough advice to students to know that unprotected sex with a new partner is dangerous sex.
"The first man I went out with after Cally left home

refused to use a condom. He said they were messy
and there was no friction. He'd never used one and
wasn't going to. We had a big fight and I told him if
he wouldn't wear one, he wasn't going to get into *my*
bed. He didn't.

"Later I realized I'd brought it up wrong. I laid it
on the line. You know. 'You want to make love to
me? You put on a condom.'

"The next man I went out with, I brought it up
gradually. I asked him if his daughter had a boyfriend.
He said, 'Lots.' I asked him what he'd told her about
AIDS, said I wanted to know what to tell Cally. That
got us talking.

"This time I didn't come on like a drill sergeant. I
told him I was scared. After all these years I thought I
was going to be free of responsibility. I was going to
be the good-time gal. Now I didn't know what to do.

"He started giving *me* a lecture on values. On being
cautious. On love. I told him I'd hardly been to bed
with any men at all, and never with someone who
used a condom. I didn't know how you did it.

"Because we'd talked about the danger, because he
knew I was anxious, he was the one who got the condoms, who made us have safe sex. *Good* sex. Neither
of us tried to pretend we knew what we were doing.
We figured out how to do it together."

Miranda, at twenty-seven, couldn't imagine anyone
not using a condom. She does. Her friends do.
They're the generation that the warnings have reached.
When I asked Miranda how she told a man she

wanted to use a condom, she looked at me as though I were crazy. "You just tell him," she said.

But some weeks later, Miranda called. "I see what you mean about condoms," she said. "I started seeing this guy from Brazil. We were in my apartment and he was about to make love to me. 'Hey, wait a sec,' I said. He hadn't put on the condom.

" 'What condom?' he said.

" 'What do you mean, what condom?' You know, it went like that. I was sort of angry. But he's from a different culture. I tried to understand. So I said, 'Halt!' and sat down on the bed and explained things to him. I told him about AIDS. As though he didn't know. But in a way, he didn't. He thought it was everyone else. I told him I didn't know if we had a future together, but that whether it was with him or without him, I wanted a future. AIDS would take it away.

"I asked him a lot of questions about what kind of AIDS information was taught in his country. We talked about being macho. We talked about our different cultures. It was great.

"We used a condom and afterward I asked, 'Was it that bad?' He said it felt maybe 20 percent less good.

"So I said he was better off making love his whole long life getting 80 percent pleasure than he would be getting 100 percent pleasure for a short time, and then getting AIDS and dying. I think I won him over."

Miranda had the conviction and the confidence to

talk to her boyfriend about condoms. She also refused to have sex with him unless he used one.

In the heat of the moment, when you hear "I hate condoms," "I can't enjoy sex wearing a rubber," "What's wrong, don't you trust me?" "Just this once . . ." would you be able to do what Miranda did? Many of us wouldn't—because we've been taught to please our partners.

In the last twenty years women have learned to take charge of our own bodies; we have learned that we have as much right to sexual pleasure as a man does. But it's been hard to learn to say "no" to unhealthy sex with a man whom we've fallen for.

Psychologists are just beginning to investigate why it's so difficult for us to protect ourselves and some are postulating that it comes down to self-esteem. One sex therapist underscored this idea when she said, "You should never feel that you are obligated to have sex to please a man. If you have developed a firm sense of who you are, that is, if you value yourself, have self-esteem, *you* are the only one who is making decisions about what you will or won't do."

One man hit on the same issue when he said, "Any woman who respects herself won't sleep around and will ask a man to use a condom. What's more important? Risking his feelings or risking your life?"

How much do you value yourself? is what he's saying. Think about it. If someone asks you to have unsafe sex, it means he isn't worrying about how you feel or how you will feel the next day—he doesn't care about you.

You're the one who must care about you. Deciding to protect yourself from AIDS is protecting your health and your body. Do you let a man decide what you'll eat, when you'll diet, whether you'll run in a marathon? Of course you don't. Bring up the condom, and bring it up early.

TALK ABOUT PRECAUTIONS
BEFORE PASSION MAKES YOU MUTE

Most women I interviewed are perfectly aware that making love with a new partner requires a condom. But most didn't know how to bring up the subject. Every man I interviewed agreed with the statement "There is always going to be awkwardness when the topic of condoms is raised." It's clear that men are just as uncomfortable as you are in broaching "the condom conversation."

One woman put it perfectly. "The subject of the condom should come up before his penis does." Without exception, men felt that the worst time to start talking about the subject is when they are already aroused.

DON'T BE ABRUPT—WORK THE
SUBJECT INTO THE CONVERSATION

A sudden question—"Do you use condoms?" "Have
you had an HIV test?"—can be seen as criticism,
as though you suspect the other person of being
both sexually dangerous and too inconsiderate to
mention it.

"Most of the time—in fact, nine times out of ten—
the male takes the lead from the female," said Dennis,
a thoughtful massage therapist. "A good way of bringing the subject up would be for the woman to say, 'I
have a problem. I need your help.' She's not asking
him to do something he doesn't want to do. She's not
saying, 'I think you might have AIDS.' She's asking
him for help. Maybe she could say something like she
had a friend who died of AIDS and that's made her
frightened. And would he help allay her fears? Would
he use a condom? Naturally, any man who would
not be sympathetic is not someone she would want
to be with."

An advertising executive from Chicago told me,
"One woman I dated was very upset about Arthur
Ashe. That started us talking about AIDS, and the
subject of condoms came up naturally. She said, 'I
went out and bought some. Do you use them?' I
hadn't, but I didn't want to admit it. It would have
made me sound stupid. Of course I knew about
AIDS. Who doesn't? But I thought it was something
that happened to other people. Her question made me

face it. When we finally went to bed together, I was wearing a condom.''

"The best way for a woman to get around the macho response or the refusal to use a condom is not to fight it,'' says Adam Glickman, the twenty-six-year-old owner of a group of condom stores. "Don't say, 'If you won't wear one, I won't go to bed with you.' That makes it a quarrel.

"Instead, if the woman says, 'Well, you feel it's not pleasurable, and I can show you a way that is,' the man gets curious and is more willing to try it. The woman can say, 'Do you know about the Japanese ones? I don't know if you realize that putting a lubricant in the tip feels very good.' The man is arguing that he doesn't want to wear one because he's convinced it won't feel good. By making it erotic, the woman gives him a way out. She says, 'You're right. That's the way it used to be. But have you tried this?' He saves face. He can say, 'Well, I haven't tried that.' ''

INSTEAD OF TELLING HIM, SHOW HIM

A man from Dallas reported that his girlfriend didn't have condoms on hand; she had them dangling from her ears. They had gone to a lecture and each time she moved her head, her large, round earrings bobbed around.

"I noticed them because they were so big—not at all her style,'' he remembered. "All through the dinner she was flirting, teasing me with these crazy earrings. Later, over coffee, she took off one of the earrings and held it out to me. I opened it up and inside was a condom. Of course I got the message." (Note: Don't use the novelty condoms, except as a way to start a conversation about safe sex. Replace them with trustworthy ones. More about which condoms to buy in the next chapter.)

Seven Ways to Bring It Up

1. "I'm glad you called. I needed cheering up. A really nice man in my office is really sick. He's the first person here to come down with AIDS. Do you work with anyone who has it?"

2. "My mother and father went to a reception at my sister's college and they were shocked because there was a big bowl of condoms on the lounge table. Like after-dinner mints. They're so out of touch. They just can't adjust to the fact that nowadays people have sex and they use condoms. Naturally!"

3. "I can't believe what a friend of mine just did. She inherited some money and she used it to buy stock in Carter-Wallace, that company that makes condoms. She said her broker recommended it since everyone needs them now."

....

4. "A young gay guy who works in our mailroom has started a pool on when TV will start showing condom ads. I said 2001. Considering all the sexy shows they put on, it's incredible that they won't run ads for condoms."

5. "Are you free Saturday afternoon?"
   "Sure, why?"
   "I wanted to go to that store that sells all those condoms, but I'm embarrassed to go alone."

6. "A friend was telling me a really sexy thing to do with a condom."
   "What was that?"
   "I can't tell you, but maybe someday I'll show you."

7. "Here's a fascinating question for you: Did you know that they've finally found something that will make you live longer?"
   "No, what is it?"
   "A condom."

four

A
Downtown
Shopping
Spree

I'm in a shopping mood," I said to a friend one Friday night after we'd had dinner together.

"What's open at ten o'clock?" he asked.

"You'll see," I told him. "Are you game to do some research for my book?"

"I've been waiting for you to ask me that," he said, grinning.

"I'm talking about *shopping*, Philip," I said firmly, smiling sweetly back at him.

We hopped in a cab and I gave the driver a downtown address. Greenwich Village had the usual weekend crowd—tourists, sailors just off a Swedish naval ship, locals walking their mutts, hip gays, college kids, the bookshop grazers, and just plain New Yorkers strolling, window-shopping and café-lounging. One store appeared to be doing a land-office business. People were coming in and out of the place at a high-intensity rate. It was exactly where Philip and I were headed.

"Condomania?" He looked inquiringly at me.

"You got it," I said. "Do you feel embarrassed going in with me?"

Macho cool, Philip responded by gallantly pushing the glass door to New York's only condom emporium wide open for me.

Inside, there was a whir of activity. Pearl Jam was coming through the loudspeaker and the store was filled with people of all ages and descriptions. The attractive young woman in lizard cowboy boots and skintight 501's at the computer cash register was ringing up sales at a brisk pace.

Philip moved off in one direction to inspect a wall of condoms; I headed to the "novelty" item area.

Browsing through the dozens of condoms packaged in every kind of plastic and cardboard, I felt as if Condomania was a cross between a candy store and a Hallmark greeting card shop. There was something for every occasion and every taste.

"If you have any questions, just let me know," said another attractive young woman. "We have two hun-

dred to choose from." She sported soft beige suede
shorts and a cream-colored silk shirt. She looked like
the fashion models we interview in our office, right
down to her red Converse high-tops. Her manner was
friendly and helpful.

"What are your best-sellers?" I asked.

"The glow-in-the-dark condom is one of the best,"
she replied, "It's for fun and games, but you can't use
them for safety. I'd suggest that you switch to another
condom if you're actually ready to use one."

"So what's safe?" I inquired.

"I'm sure you know that even a condom can't be
guaranteed to be 100 percent safe," she responded,
"but major American brands are carefully tested for
disease prevention. They sell the most, but the new
Japanese ones from firms like Sagami and Okamoto
are excellent and we sell a lot of them, too."

"Why's that?"

"They're supposedly thinner and silkier," she said.

"Have you tried them?" I asked.

"They do look sheerer. My boyfriend and I used
some, but we didn't see that big of a difference," she
said matter-of-factly.

"Tell me about the 'novelty' condoms," I said.

"Well, as you can see, we have a tremendous selec-
tion. But if you look at the label, you'll see there are
warnings saying they're not effective against HIV."

A bowl of walnuts was next to the novelty racks
and I picked one up.

"That's a real walnut shell," the young woman said,

"but when you crack it open you find a condom. It's another one of those that are only for fun."

Philip had sauntered over and I showed the walnut to him.

"Buy a bowl of them," he advised with a straight face.

"Did you learn anything new?" I asked him.

"Yes," he replied. "Cool. Very cool. Condoms from around the world, for everyone in the world. This is really a fun place."

"That's what everyone says," the young woman agreed, as Philip did a discreet double take when he took in her long, tawny legs.

"So what are you buying?" I asked him.

"Miss, where are the magnums?" he asked the saleswoman. He grinned before giving me a look.

"Oh, you should buy several to see what feels best," she responded with a warm but businesslike smile.

Philip chose a Texas-manufactured Stealth condom—black, cool ("They'll never see you coming!"), but unsafe—and one German and one Japanese brand. I purchased a dozen walnuts.

From its earliest days, the condom has had an image problem. While there are hints of condom usage in ancient Egypt and Rome, its first definite appearance was in the sixteenth century. The design came from Gabriel Fallopius, a doctor who studied the reproductive organs and whose memory is honored inside each

of us via the fallopian tubes. Fallopius's sheath of
medicated linen covering the tip of the penis was
meant to be protective. When a man slid it on, he was
usually about to have sex with a woman who was not
quite acceptable.

Later, the condom began to cover the whole penis
and was made, variously, out of animal gut or fish
membrane. Nevertheless, it still acted, in the words of
the Marquise de Sevigne, as "armour against love, gos-
samer against infection." Forsaking such protestations,
Casanova, in the following century, was among the
first to popularize the condom for contraceptive use.

By the mid-nineteenth century, the condom was
made out of rubber, and with the introduction of
thinner latex in the 1930s, it became less uncomfortable and its efficiency improved; its image didn't.

A sock, a French letter, a raincoat, a bag, a rubber—these are some of the slang terms for the condom. Somewhere along the way, donning a raincoat or
posting a French letter also became a handy way of
blocking pregnancy. But even though the man might
be using a condom with a woman he loved, usually,
when he put one on, it was because he was about to
have illicit sex or unmarried sex—sex, which in the
eyes of society, he should not be having at all.

Like books bought in brown-paper wrappers, the
condom was not nice. It was a naughty little packet
sold from a vending machine in the men's room of
the local gas station, and because it partook of the for-
bidden, it came to be seen as a mark of manhood.

Small wonder that the condom's reputation can make even the most intelligent woman embarrassed about practicing safe sex. The new generation of marketing merchants is trying to improve things. Condoms like the Stealth that my pal Philip bought have great promotional potential and maybe men will respond to ads like the one I heard recently on the radio, reminding listeners that "there's always time to dress for the occasion . . . slip into a Tuxedo." The announcer was not referring to a dress suit; he was promoting a new brand of condoms.

The *Wall Street Journal* reported a few years ago that in France, thirty-one artists from eight European countries had produced comic strips called "The Adventure of Latex." The first Condomania store opened in 1991 and there are already eight—and many more planned—across America.

The most interesting news in condoms, however, is the female condom that may soon be sanctioned by the FDA. Manufactured by Wisconsin Pharmaceutical Company, the product consists of a lubricated polyurethane sheath with a flexible polyurethane ring on each end. One ring is inserted into the vagina much like a diaphragm; the other remains outside, partially covering the labia.

A colleague of mine describes the female condom, which will be marketed under the trade name Reality, as "big enough to catch Texas rainwater." Among the condom's drawbacks are a high failure rate for pregnancy and for preventing STDs and HIV transmission.

As of January 1993, the condom has not been FDA approved, but if and when it is, women would be well advised to use it with a spermicidal lubricant.

The Condom Connoisseur

Even if the man in your life buys and supplies the condoms, every woman should know how to use them and how to choose them.

Condoms are made out of either lambskin or latex. The former, while providing more sensation, do not provide protection against infection. The walls are more porous than latex and sometimes leak. If you buy a condom, make sure that it is made of latex. You don't need those condoms labeled extra-strength. For vaginal intercourse and oral sex, a regular condom will provide the necessary safety.

Currently three companies dominate the condom market: Carter-Wallace manufactures Trojans; Schmid Laboratories makes Ramses and Sheik condoms; and Ansell-Americas is the manufacturer of Lifestyles. There are also many other condom manufacturers in Europe and new, smaller ones in the United States, but those three companies produce the most popular condoms, so you are most likely to find them in the drugstore. When choosing condoms, always look for those that are specifically labeled as being for prevention of pregnancy and protection against disease.

The FDA checks the quality of condoms before they can be sold in the United States or imported from abroad. The rule is that 99.6 percent of a given batch must pass leakage tests or the whole lot is dumped. In theory, this means four condoms out of every thousand may leak, so it is extra-important to use a spermicidal lubricant with condoms at all times. The reason for using a spermicidal lubricant is that you get a greater degree of protection against pregnancy, STDs, and HIV.

To make shopping simpler, look for spermicidal lubricants that contain nonoxynol-9 because it wipes out sperm as well as the organisms responsible for many STDs. In the lab, nonoxynol-9 has killed HIV, but using it in a test tube is different from a vagina, so the best protection is the condom and nonoxynol-9 together to prevent disease and pregnancy.

I wish I could say definitively that health experts estimate that using a condom with nonoxynol-9 according to instructions gives 100 percent protection against the HIV virus, but the research is often confusing and, to date, there are no clear or consistent percentages available that make complete sense. But the two together are, at present, our best defense against HIV transmission and STDs.

One final note: in order for nonoxynol-9 to be effective against disease and pregnancy, it must remain in the vagina for at least six hours. Do not douche after sex. You will wash away your protection.

WET OR DRY?

The type of condom you choose—plain, lubricated, lubricated with spermicide, or flavored—will depend on your sexual preferences and plans.

Some condoms are sold already lubricated, some are not. Lubricants come two ways: those containing spermicide (usually nonoxynol-9) and those that do not. The condom you buy should be labeled with the type of lubricant it contains. As you will see, there are uses for both kinds of lubricants.

Nonlubricated condoms are preferred by most men for oral sex. (In a later chapter you'll find detailed step-by-step instructions for having oral sex with a condom.) Unadulterated latex tastes terrible, so your best bet is using a flavored condom (many women like mint best). If you want to use a lubricant during oral sex, then you might opt for ForPlay Sensual Succulents, a line of harmless, water-based lubricants with all-natural flavorings.

One of the research editors for this book gathered a group of friends and *Self* staffers for a ForPlay flavor test. The results: Thumbs up to Au'Natural, Green Apple, Warm Cinnamon, and Passion Fruit, thumbs down to Mandarin Orange ("a resounding no," was one response), French Vanilla, and Cool Citrus.

Whether you choose to use a lubricant for oral sex or not, during intercourse there is no substitute for a lubricant containing nonoxynol-9.

If you are having oral sex and switch to intercourse,

change to a nonoxynol-9 lubricated condom or add nonoxynol-9 lubricant to the condom you're using.

One more note on lubricants: Always use a *water-based* lubricant. Some people, to ease entry with a nonlubricated condom, smear it with oil or an oil-based cream. Wrong on two counts: *Oil dissolves the latex! And, for intercourse, condoms should always be used with water-based nonoxynol-9 lubricants.*

Here's some information you need on the subject:

"YES" TO WATER-BASED LUBRICANTS

Some of the brands listed below (ForPlay, for example) are available with and without nonoxynol-9. Some companies that currently make water-based lubricants without nonoxynol-9 are developing new products that include it, so to be sure of exactly what your lubricant contains, check the label carefully.

KY
ForPlay
Cornhuskers Lotion
Today Personal Lubricant
Surgilube
any water-based vaginal jelly
Astroglide

"NO" TO OIL-BASED LUBRICANTS

None of the following contains nonoxynol-9, and all of them are harmful to the latex that condoms are made of.

mineral oil
baby oil
petroleum jelly (such as Vaseline)
hand lotions
body lotions
vegetable or olive oil

HOW BIG IS BIG?

There is a story told that during World War II Winston Churchill commissioned a condom manufacturer to make enormous condoms and put them in crates marked AVERAGE-SIZE. The air force then dropped them over Germany. The same psychology is at work today when condom manufacturers size their products.

No company makes a "small." There is "regular," which is somewhere between seven and seven and three-quarters inches long. Most condoms are regulars and the package isn't marked with any special indication of size. "Maxx," "Maxx Plus," and "Magnum" denote the largest sizes, between eight and eight and a quarter inches. And where a company manufacturing items for a less sensitive part of the anatomy might label their product "small," condom manufacturers use a more euphemistic name, such as in Lifestyles Snugger Fit, an item that's a little over six and a half inches long.

If you are buying the condoms, which size should you choose? Unless you have reason to believe that your lover far exceeds the average penis size of six and a half inches, buy a regular.

There are also two different shapes in condoms, straight-walled and contoured. Some men find the latter more comfortable than the former, since they follow the shape of the penis. But most stores carry straight-walled, and since you probably don't want to describe the shape of your lover's penis to the clerk, if the man in your life wants contoured, let him buy the condoms himself.

IF HE'S JEALOUS, CHOOSE GREEN

Condoms now come in colors. Lots of them. Does it make sex feel better? No. Is it fun? Yes. A penis looks very different when clad in a thin layer of blue latex than it does when it's covered with green. The FDA cautions against using black condoms. The dye may be a carcinogen and could rub off. Usually colored condoms do not provide protection against AIDS. To be safe when you're buying a colored condom, make sure the label says it's for prevention of STDs and AIDS.

WHEN A CONDOM HAS PASSED ITS PRIME

Condoms deteriorate after about two years. Some packages display the date of manufacture so you can determine how old they are. Condoms that are lubricated with spermicide must, by law, have an expiration date, so always check it.

Keep condoms in a cool dry place away from sunlight. Note: Even though glove compartments are handy, don't use them for storage, as they suffer from temperature extremes. If you've opened a condom package and find that it's gummy as opposed to slick, which is appropriate for a lubricated type, or it is brittle or has holes or slits, the condom is no good.

When you remove one from a package, be careful not to tear it. This means you should *not* attack the wrapping in a lustful frenzy when it proves hard to open. And if you are cultivating a set of Dragon Lady fingernails, be careful they don't catch on the condom when you are putting it on your lover's penis.

TICKLING HER FANCY

What about the condoms that proclaim themselves "dotted," "ribbed," or otherwise enhanced with humps, bumps, and other protrusions, all of which supposedly enhance a woman's pleasure by providing additional stimulation for the clitoris? They don't. A hump, a bump, or a rib would have to protrude more than these do to provide any extra sensation, either pleasant or painful. There's no danger in them, but no added physical satisfaction either, though the playfulness of using one can stimulate the imagination and make the encounter more erotic.

five

Making Sexy Love, Nineties Style

When you buy a package of condoms, you'll find that each one is individually sealed in its own tinfoil or plastic packet. Most have serrated edges and are easy to tear open. If you do have difficulty, make a small cut in the edge with a nail scissors, being careful not to damage the latex inside. Do this *before* you and your lover get into bed. Urgency can make you careless.

Each package also comes with simple instructions on how to use them. Here's a synopsis of the basic materials:

1. *Leaving Room at the Top.* Although some condoms simply have a rounded top, many more now have a small, nipplelike protrusion. This reservoir is there to collect the semen and keep it from running down the penis when a man ejaculates. Whether or not there is a reservoir, pinch a half-inch at the top of the condom before you begin to roll it down over the penis. This keeps air from being trapped in the condom and gives the man's ejaculate someplace to go.

2. *The Roll Down.* The condom, which emerges flat from its packet, will, once you have pinched air out of the top, look a little like a latex beanie. If your lover would like you to put it on his penis for him (for more about when and if he wants you to, see page 56), fit the condom over his erection and roll it down until the condom has reached the base of his penis. If it stops short, the condom is too small; the man in your life is a Maxx.

3. *Take It Off.* After ejaculation, the man should withdraw, holding the condom in place at the base of his penis so that it will not slip off. The condom is more likely to slip off if the man has gone entirely limp. This means that the postcoital catnap, with the penis still inside the vagina, is not a good idea. As soon as he has withdrawn, the condom should be carefully removed, dis-

posed of in the toilet or a wastebasket, and the man should wash both his penis and his hands.

Although those are the basic instructions and precautions you'll receive packaged along with condoms, I found in my travels that many women had questions that condom manufacturers *don't* deal with. Following are things they never thought to tell you.

CAN YOU PUT A CONDOM ON A PENIS WHEN IT'S FLACCID?

Not if it's entirely limp, but if the man has a partial erection, you can. As you begin to roll the condom down, the partial erection usually becomes total. Remember that there must be an air space at the top to catch the semen, and that the condom must reach the base of the penis.

WHAT DOES ORAL SEX FEEL LIKE WHEN A MAN WEARS A CONDOM?

It can feel very pleasurable for both of you. Details on this in Chapter Seven.

I HEARD THERE'S A "WOMAN'S CONDOM," CALLED A DENTAL DAM. WHAT IS IT FOR?

A dental dam and a condom for women are two separate items. The female condom was described in the previous chapter. There are mixed opinions as to whether a dental dam is necessary, but some doctors recommend that if a woman is at high risk, her vaginal area should be protected with a dental dam when she's receiving oral sex. This item is a square of thick latex about six by six inches, sold by dental supply stores and sometimes used to protect a patient's mouth during drilling.

Dental dams are now being sold in stores that specialize in condoms, and the manufacturers have tried to make them look as though they belong in the bedroom, turning them out in delightfully decadent colors like mauve. They *look* like they might feel good, but they don't. The material used to make the dental dam is thicker than that used in condoms. It is also opaque.

"I felt like I should have had a compass," was the way one man described trying to perform oral sex on a woman protected with a dental dam. And a woman's reaction? "I couldn't feel a thing. Until they come out with a thinner 'woman's condom,' I'll keep doing what I do. I take a regular man's condom, cut it down one side so that I can open it up and spread it over my vulva."

DOES SEX FEEL AS GOOD
WITH A CONDOM?

Every man I talked to said there was less sensation with a condom, some putting it as low as 60 percent of the pleasure they would feel if they were not similarly sheathed, others saying that they would rate the condom in the 90 percent range. "There's an insulation there," said one. "You don't get the same bite."

Humorist Roy Blount, Jr., concurs: "Wearing a condom is not nearly as much fun as being nekkid nekkid nekkid."

Despite the universal agreement that condoms cause some loss of sensation, no man I interviewed denied the need for them. And some men said that they had discovered increased pleasure through more imaginative foreplay. "I guess you could say that the condom has taught me to compensate," said one man. "Originally I thought of it as losing sexual satisfaction. Now I think of it as forcing me to focus on other sensual pleasures."

Condom Cautions

DON'T OFFER A NEW LOVER
AN OLD PACKAGE OF CONDOMS

"The night Jean and I first made love, she reached into the drawer of her night table and took out a box of condoms," said Stewart. "I was glad she had them on hand. Then later I got to thinking about it. What if the package had already been opened? I would have felt jealous. I would have wondered who had used the other ones." The moral here: Keep fresh boxes of condoms on hand, or empty them into a bedside drawer before you need them.

DON'T AUTOMATICALLY GIVE A HELPING HAND

Some men find it sexy when a woman helps to put on the condom. "Most men would find it a turn-on if she just made it part of the lovemaking," said one professional baseball player.

Other men disagree. "I don't really like using a condom," said Gary. "When my girlfriend puts it on, it takes too long. I want to get it on fast, before I lose my erection."

"Advise your readers never to even ask to put a condom on a man the first time you go to bed together," said one man emphatically. "I've found that women never put it on right, I have to adjust it. Let the man do it until you've been with him several times."

Another man counseled: "The less attention focused on putting it on, the better. It's a downer. Take as little time with it as possible until you know each other real well."

"You're holding hands, you kiss, you get naked," explained a sexy guy from Cleveland, "and *pow!*

you've got to put the damn thing on. But in five years condoms will be mainstreamed. They'll be an integrated part of the act. So get used to it."

"Are you ready for this?' another man inquired during a phone interview we had. "My girlfriend sometimes puts a condom on me with her mouth. It's awesome!" (More on this maneuver in Chapter 7.)

NEVER REUSE A CONDOM

Each time a man ejaculates, he must use a new condom. It cannot be cleaned off and used again. If your lover does not dispose of the condom as soon as he has an orgasm, ask him to do so. Make sure he uses a fresh one if he reenters you. And *never* let a man continue to wear the same condom for vaginal sex that he has just used for anal intercourse.

CONDOMS CAN CAUSE TEMPORARY IMPOTENCE

An erection can be a fragile thing and men worry about losing it. Suggest too bluntly that you want to take that fragile thing and sheath it in latex and some men go limp. "The more anxious you are about your performance, the more problems you're going to have," said one man. "The more paraphernalia you have, the more anxious you're going to be."

Some men may also fail to get an erection because they're feeling resentful about having to use a condom. Several men I talked with advised that the best way to deal with condom-caused impotence is to make the condom part of foreplay, turning it into a pleasure rather than a penance. Buy different kinds and experiment. Unroll them, play at putting them on his penis—and keep your sense of humor. When your sexual relations resume their natural course, his penis will, too.

CONDOMS CAN HELP TO PREVENT PREMATURE EJACULATION

If a man reaches climax too quickly, using a condom can be a boon. Because the condom slightly decreases sensation, men who have been subject to premature ejaculation find that wearing one enables them to maintain an erection for a longer time.

Although the majority of men would prefer to go "nekkid, nekkid, nekkid," once you both acknowledge that making love in the Nineties includes the condom, you'll find that sex is just as fervent and just as exciting as it ever was.

six

Love
Without
Latex

M ost people believe that when you finally settle
down with a single sex partner, you can let
the latex go.

Maybe. But as with everything else that has to do
with AIDS, this is a decision that no one can make
for you.

Some researchers who take the extreme position are
aware of the often shaky communication that exists
between lovers, and they say to be truly safe, you can
never give up the condom. Others suggest that you
look at your life honestly, and if you think that there
is little or no risk, put the condom away.

They all counsel that before you reject the condom, you should be sure that neither you nor your partner is carrying the HIV virus.

This means that before abandoning the protection of the condom, both parties should be tested for the HIV virus.

"Potential sexual partners should be considered infected until proven otherwise," says William A. Haseltine, scientist and chief of retrovirus research at Harvard's Dana-Farber Cancer Institute. "A lot of people don't want to address what the risks mean in terms of behavior. It isn't comfortable to think like this, but these are the realities we face today. . . . You want my personal advice? Don't have sex with anybody unless you've had them tested."

Assuming that, after the six-month waiting period, the test results are negative, are your fears of AIDS then over?

Well, not quite. AIDS has made both men and women take a hard look at the question of fidelity.

AIDS and the Extramarital Affair

"The question of when to stop using the condom rests on a matter of trust," says the CDC's AIDS hot line. "Couples have to realize that in being unfaithful today they're risking more than the other person's feelings."

A general practitioner in New York City says he finds it very hard to counsel patients on when they can stop using a condom. "It's a difficult question to answer. I have one satyr of a patient who comes in to be tested every six months. He'll sleep with anything that will take its pants off.

"I have another patient, a thirty-year-old guy, who just this week got drunk in the bar where he works, and one of the lady customers gave him an offer he couldn't refuse. They had oral sex right there in the bar. He's got a monogamous relationship otherwise. He's been with his partner for seven months. They're still in the condom stage, but she wants to stop using one. Now, the chances of spreading AIDS through oral sex are slight, but he didn't know this woman at all. He had no idea what kind of life she led. I told him to be perfectly safe, he'd better stick with the condom."

Note that the bartender hadn't told his partner about his defection. Such sexual slips often slip the mind of the man who made them. When *Glamour* magazine polled a thousand men on how they felt about various aspects of sex, 37 percent confessed to having lied to at least one woman about their sexual fidelity. An additional 25 percent said that they had lied about a secret vice. Maybe the vice was an addiction to Oreo cookies. Maybe it was something more dangerous.

If AIDS has taught us that we must learn to communicate in order to use a condom, it is also teaching us that communication is vitally important if we want to stop using one. We have to take a good look at our partners and be honest with ourselves about what we see. "It is a question of trust, but love has always been a question of trust," says a young man in New Mexico who recently moved in with his girlfriend. "We had the test before we moved in together. Since then we haven't used condoms."

Partners who can't talk to each other, who refuse to confront their fears or discuss their infidelities, put themselves at risk from AIDS. When it actually comes to telling a lover that you've been unfaithful and didn't use a condom, the ultimate question is: Are you so worried about hurting your partner's feelings that you're willing to risk his or her life?

The day has passed when someone can turn a blind eye to a partner who plays around. Yes, confrontation may cause a crisis in the marriage or an intimate relationship. How do you tell your husband or lover that from now on he must use a condom when making love to you unless you acknowledge his—or your— infidelity? Avoiding the issue, turning a blind eye, as so many women have done in the past, is now too dangerous.

Almost every man I talked to, when asked how he would deal with the AIDS issue if he began to suspect that his partner was unfaithful, said he would definitely bring it up.

Even though most women said the same, among those I asked were two whose mates are notorious skirt chasers. Obviously, they *hadn't* brought it up. They were still denying what was going on. Despite evidence to the contrary, both these women preferred to preserve the belief that their partners were faithful. This head-in-the-sand attitude is more common among older women, who may be financially dependent on their husband's support or think they need to preserve the marriage at all costs. But that cost is now too high.

Any woman who suspects that her mate is playing around should immediately seek professional advice on how to deal with the issue of AIDS.

A marriage counselor or family therapist can help you acknowledge that you are in a marriage that does not include fidelity and to insist on protected sex. The up side: Therapists today concur that bringing unfaithfulness out of the closet may open up real communication between partners who have been emotional strangers for years and enable them to put their marriage on a new and positive footing.

Part Two
Being Sexy

seven

The
Seduction
Dinner

When we enter a room where the candles are lit and the table is set for two, we know that we are being courted. We are flattered by the flickering light, soothed by soft music. We let down our defenses and give ourselves over to the anticipation of pleasure.

I am a great believer in that old adage "The way to a man's heart is through his stomach." The dinner that is meant to seduce and enthrall traditionally has included champagne, oysters, lobster, exquisite chocolate cakes. Why? Foods that are as rich as they are rare and tasty signal to the seducee that he/she is being treated in a very special way.

The seduction dinner works because it's based on a sound psychological principle: *nurturing*. There's hardly a human who can resist being taken care of, who doesn't appreciate the fact that someone took the time and thought to prepare a meal especially for him.

"No one's ever invited me to a wildly romantic dinner," said an artist who lives in Santa Fe. "I'd love it!' So would a great many other men.

A friend who lives in London says, "I've invited a lot of women to seduction dinners, but I am sorry to report that no woman has ever invited me. It would be so easy. You could have me for a lettuce leaf."

Exotic truffles and expensive foie gras are not necessary elements of the romantic dinner. Neither should you settle for serving a lettuce leaf. Ingenuity is the name of the seduction game. Dinners can be formal with your best china and crystal, or they can be picnics served on the floor. If you eschew cooking, you can always order a pizza, serve it up with candles on a pretty cloth, and add a bottle of champagne.

Menus should be both simple and full of flavors that tantalize the taste. Too heavy a meal and too much alcohol will put you both to sleep. Too complicated a meal will interfere with romance, for what is the point of all that atmosphere if he is in one room and you are stirring pots in another?

One woman I know told me that she serves a romantic meal in her candlelit kitchen, and while she stands at the stove she hands her man a book of her favorite poems, asking him to read aloud while she prepares dinner. "I discovered years ago," she says, "that in the right surroundings reading aloud—or being read to—can set a very intimate and romantic mood."

She forgoes her usual low-cholesterol regimen as she breaks eggs in a bowl, mixes them with cream, melts butter in a saucepan and begins cooking the eggs slowly over low heat, stirring to keep them from sticking. She toasts two slices of bread and butters them. When the eggs are the consistency of a rich, golden custard, she spoons them onto the toast and tops them with mounds of black caviar. Served with a bottle of ice-cold wine or chilled vodka in glasses frosted in the freezer, it is a meal, she says, that soothes as it seduces.

She does not leave it at that. She said that she once read that chocolate contains phenylethylamine (PEA), a substance that gives us the rush of excitement we associate with romance. Leaving nothing to chance, when the eggs have been eaten, she brings out dessert, a platter on which she has stuffed every kind of chocolate she could buy—chocolate chip cookies and chocolate brownies, chocolate truffles and chocolate mints, and chocolate fudge.

"If romance doesn't work," she says philosophically, "we can binge on chocolate."

Deborah, my friend from Los Angeles, espouses the stomach-to-heart wisdom, too. But she firmly believes you don't have to buy or prepare a whole dinner. All you need is an Italian Parma ham.

"When I was visiting friends in Italy, I noticed that there was always a beautiful Parma ham on the kitchen counter. It was placed in a special stand so that you could carve it easily. My hostess told me that men appreciate having food around the house. Her husband and his friends would always head toward the kitchen to gnosh on the Parma.

"When I got back to New York, I wanted to rekindle some flames with my boyfriend. I splurged on half of a prosciutto ham, which is the closest thing I could find to Parma—Smithfield ham is almost as good—and some great Italian bread. When Henry came over I led him to the kitchen. He immediately started nibbling. I put out some olives, a bottle of cold cider, and lit some candles. He knew something was going on.

"We had a fabulous reunion. And the ham keeps for weeks!"

When the seduction supper—or the nibbling—is over, leave any dishes undone. "A woman who's more into the pots and pans than she is to me sends a warning signal," says a thirty-two-year-old. "Her priorities are elsewhere. That kills it all."

So once you're settled down in the living room, you're ready for The Kiss.

The Kiss

In the days before the Pill and MTV, there was almost nothing sexier than a kiss. It was the first romantic contact most of us ever had, that moment under the mistletoe or beneath the light of a silvery moon when a casual flirtation became something more.

Kisses are an introduction, the way we begin to sense someone with our bodies instead of trying to know them with our minds.

Men can still be swayed by a kiss.

"A romantic kiss," says someone close to me, "is soft and so vulnerable. Inviting. Passionate. And wet. Dry kisses are simply functional."

"One of my best memories is the music of Vivaldi and kissing nonstop for two of *The Four Seasons*," says one man. Another man who extols kissing reports that "the sexiest experience I ever had was an endless kiss. We began kissing, then we just relaxed into each other, lying mouth to mouth, breathing together, tongues sometimes touching, sometimes not. We did this for hours. When we finally moved apart I felt as though I had been one and now I was only a half. I felt severed."

These men are not so unusual in their views: 58 percent of the thousand men surveyed recently by *Glamour* magazine said that given a choice between a great, intensely erotic kiss or so-so intercourse, they'd prefer the kiss.

How do you give an intensely erotic kiss? A man in his mid-twenties described it like this:

"A great kiss is not rigid, it's anticipatory. Even before you reach out for her, the woman has her mouth slightly open. She's begun the kiss before you get there. Then you put your lips on hers and a really sexy woman will meet you with her mouth wide open. With a sexy woman a kiss is communication, an invitation. . . ."

Arousing Him

Even though most of us enjoy surveying an attractive male backside in a pair of Calvins, I'm amazed at how many women reveal their ignorance of a man's body. And I'm not talking about sixteen-year-olds. Experienced women who have been married or have had various lovers think that once you've learned to stroke a penis, you have a doctorate from the school of love.

No man will deny the pleasures of his penis, but there are many other areas of sensitivity on his body. The deepest sexual pleasures come from a heightened sensuality, and to achieve that, we also need to pay attention to the rest of the skin that covers him. To know how to please, you have to know what you're touching. To understand your lover's body, you must explore it.

When I asked a thirty-two-year-old to describe his favorite sexual fantasy, he said this: "Slowly undressing and being undressed by a woman, looking at each other, touching each other over our entire bodies before finally touching the genitals. Then having oral sex. And only then going on to intercourse."

Tell the man in your life that you are going to introduce him to the game of touch.

Tell him that anatomy is destiny.

Tell him you are going to take off his tie.

How many times have you seen a man walk into a room and reach up his hand to pull off his tie? It is the gesture men use to declare themselves free of the workaday world. As you raise your hands to free him, he will begin to help.

Say no, and push his hands aside. Explain that you want to take your time, to enjoy the sight of him, and that when he is naked, he may do the same to you.

Move slowly. Not all destinations should be reached in record time. When we go too fast, we miss the pleasures along the way.

Slip his shirttail out of his pants, finish unbuttoning his shirt, and slide it off his shoulders. Unfasten the cuffs and pull his sleeves down, freeing his arms and hands and letting the shirt drop to the floor.

Now begin to explore. Weigh his hand in yours. Run your tongue across his palm, and then feather your fingers over the back of his hand, where the fine filaments of hair are particularly sensitive to a light, teasing touch. This is the hand that will please you, that will touch your breasts and slide down between your legs.

Now put his fingers in your mouth one by one, licking, tasting, and stroking. Run your tongue and your hands up his arms, exploring your way to his shoulders.

He will try to reciprocate. Don't let him. Tell him that if he will accept your curiosity, you will later welcome his. After you have explored his hands, his arms, his chest, ask him to sit down. Take off his shoes and socks and begin to touch his feet, tracing the sole of each foot with your fingers, feeling the shape and weight of his foot in your hand, stroking each of his toes. Toes are sensitive to the touch, though we rarely think of them as spots of possible sensual pleasure.

Now unbuckle his belt, slide down his pants, and run your hands over his back, tracing the path his spine follows from the nape of his neck to the beginning of his buttocks. Press the tips of your fingers around the base of his neck, over his shoulders. You'll feel where his muscles have tightened into knots. Massage lightly, easing his tensions, helping him to unwind.

By this time, unless he is extremely tense or very wary, he will have relaxed into the physical sensations he's experiencing. Slip off his underwear, caress his thighs, his legs, his arms, his chest—everywhere *but* his penis. *Then*—when you're ready to stroke his penis—you're ready for the condom.

The Ultimate Condom Trick

Putting a condom on your lover with your mouth is a very sexy thing to do. I'd heard that professionals are skilled in this art, but none of the women I interviewed knew the specifics of technique. Then I came across a man who told me that his lover had surprised him by putting a condom on him with her mouth. He gave me her name, Suzanne, and upon telephoning her, I was given the definitive how-to. Here is what she told me.

"The choice of condom is all-important and taste governs that decision. The one I prefer is unlubricated and mint-scented, because it tastes best. All the others I've tried have a distinct flavor of latex, and the spermicide ones are positively gagging. When I first put one of those in my mouth and I literally had to run for the Listerine.

"This is how you do what I call 'the ultimate condom trick.' Make sure your mouth is very wet. Keep a glass of water by the bed in case your mouth should get dry. As soon as your lover has an erection, open the packet that contains a mint-scented condom. Keep in mind that you will be unrolling the condom on the penis in the same way you'd roll a woolen cap down on your head and over your ears.

"Suck the nipple end into your mouth anchoring the nipple against the roof of your mouth with your tongue. (Most condoms have a nipple or reservoir tip for semen. If you are not using one with a lengthened top, flatten about half an inch of the condom with your tongue, as above.)

"Now place the entire condom in your mouth so that it is positioned between your lips and your front teeth. If you were to take an X-ray of this you'd see the flat circle of the condom in front of your teeth behind your lips. Flatten the nipple with the tip of your tongue, keeping it affixed to the top of your mouth until you begin moving down on his penis. This is key because if there's air in the condom it may break.

"Now, gently encircling the shaft of his penis with one hand and the thumb and forefinger of the other so that only the head and an inch or so below it is uncovered, place your mouth with the entire condom in it on the head of the penis. As soon as you have done this, immediately slide your lips behind the ring of the condom so you are now pressing the condom against the head of the penis with your mouth. With the nipple end still inside your mouth and the ring outside and flat against your lips, you can slip the condom down over the head of the penis. Your lips should firmly push the ring of the condom down the penis as far as your mouth will go. Then, using your hands, slide the rest of the condom down to the base of the penis.

"Many men lose some of their erection when putting a condom on. If you feel him start to go limp, lick his pubic hair, softly stroke his testicles with your tongue, and use your hand to stimulate him again.

"You'll probably need a few practice sessions

before you get the hang of this technique. But very few men will complain at this kind of experimentation, especially if you make the experience pleasurable by using your hands in sensuous ways while trying to master the skill with your mouth. *And* if you keep your sense of humor."

Suzanne left out one valuable step in her fascinating instructions. She neglected to mention putting a dab of nonoxynol-9 lubricant inside the tip of the condom. This makes it more comfortable for him and adds more protection for you.

Incidentally, Suzanne is not the only one who has been experimenting. I had heard whisperings about groups that have been organized to "heighten the eroticism of latex," and recently, an indefatigable research editor tracked down a course entitled "A Sexological Health Perspective" at the Institute for the Advanced Study of Human Sexuality in San Francisco. This class was designed, in part, to help students "eroticize sexual health" with "experiential approaches." Participants are taught how to put on a condom anally— another first for San Francisco, America's sexual pacesetter.

Oral Sex, Nineties Style

In 1982 when I talked about *How to Make Love to a Man* on TV talk shows, I avoided all mention of "oral sex" and alluded to it as "the most intimate act," hoping the viewers would get my drift. Today the media is unembarrassed about oral sex and I'd certainly get flack if I referred to any one sexual experience as the "most intimate act."

Somewhere in the Eighties, oral sex turned from an unmentionable near-taboo to a fundamental given of sexual life. The majority of men I talk with in the Nineties agree that oral sex is now a requisite ingredient in making love. "It's expanded the sexual boundaries," says a thirty-six-year-old single man. "Usually when I first had sex with someone it was in the missionary position. Now I find that women are pretty eager to give a man oral sex. A few years ago, in my experience, women had to be coaxed."

Oral sex was important to men when I wrote about it in 1982, and men love it just as much today. Why? Because it feels good physically and makes a man feel good psychologically.

"It's the most intimate thing a woman can do for me," said one man. "She is acknowledging my penis with her mouth. There's something incredibly trusting about that."

"It reinforces my masculinity and gives me a feeling of control," explained another man. "A woman may think she's controlling the man, but the man really feels that she is being submissive to him—and that's something that I can't deny is exciting to me."

If you've mastered putting a condom on a man with your mouth, oral sex is a cinch. I described the technique in my first book but before I give you an updated Nineties version, here's a terrific tip from a woman I sat next to in a gynecologist's office.

"I've got to give a testimonial to Astroglide," she declared. "Believe it or not I heard about it from one of the world's best-known women—a TV news personality. She was talking to some of her friends at a party and I was standing at the edge of the group, listening with all ears. She was absolutely correct. Astroglide is the greatest lubricant. It feels like natural fluids, but in a way is slipperier and, if you can believe it, makes sex even better. Anyway, put a couple of drops of Astroglide on your hands and you'll love it when you have oral sex. It tastes faintly sweet. And of course it's perfect for regular sex too."

There are a few subtle differences in oral sex when he is using a condom. You will feel a small, crinkled-up nipple of latex in your mouth. This is not an unpleasant sensation but one that is simply different. Some women report that they have the feeling that the condom might come off in the mouth as they move up and down on the penis shaft. This doesn't happen. A condom is designed for a tight fit, and even relatively firm tugging doesn't dislodge it. Using a lubricant makes the up-and-down movement of hands and lips easier and gives added sensation.

Now, here's the complete step-by-step:

If you think of your mouth as the opening of a vagina and think of your hands as an extension of your mouth when you encircle the shaft of the penis, you'll be able to use them to give the most pleasure. Begin by licking his penis, keeping it well lubricated with saliva (or a few drops of lubricant). Make your tongue as sharp and pointed as you can and gently probe the areas around the most sensitive part, the head. If, at this point—or any other time—your thoughts stray or you feel anxious, *concentrate totally* on what you are doing with your hands and mouth.

Now lick and stroke the penis, concentrating on the ridge that runs down the center of the underside. (This ridge is clearly visible through a condom.) Keeping your tongue pointed, lightly flick it back and forth on the little edge of skin where the head is joined to the shaft—for many men this is the most sensitive and responsive part of the penis. You may want to kiss or stroke it lengthwise with your tongue. Remember to relax, remember to breathe, and focus on the fact that you are giving pleasure. Make your tongue and lip movements firm, because latex diminishes sensation.

Now return to where the head and shaft connect. Take your time but don't hesitate: Make smooth, fluid movements. You can envelop the penis with your mouth in a tight oval, lips drawn back, covering your teeth. Rest the penis on your tongue. The all-important oral friction now begins in which your mouth and tongue imitate the reciprocal motion and kneading action of the vagina. Move your mouth back and forth, up and down on the penis, constantly keeping in mind that your lips and mouth should feel like a very snug vagina. Begin slowly and increase your speed subtly at every forward stroke. The important point to remember here is that you are not sucking on the penis, but slowly moving up and down the shaft while keeping the head of the penis in your mouth.

There seem to be two schools of thought about

what is most pleasurable in oral sex. Some men contend that the more length taken into the mouth, the more satisfying it is to them. If your partner is in this group, you might be interested to know that the trick Linda Lovelace used in the classic X-rated film *Deep Throat* was to throw her head back off the edge of a bed so that her mouth formed one long passage. If you have a tendency to gag because he begins to thrust or your throat can't accommodate enough of his penis, take a second's pause, breathe deeply to relax your muscles and continue on. If the problem persists, encircle part of the shaft with your hand to block his complete thrust.

Another contingent of men feels that the head of the penis is the most sensitive area and the mouth need cover only that area plus one or two inches down the shaft. If your lover or husband is in this group, then use one of your hands as an extension of your mouth. Make a snug circle around the penis with your thumb and forefinger, keeping your lips in contact with your fingers. Now move your hand up and down the shaft of the penis in the same rhythm as your mouth. As your mouth goes down on the shaft, your hand moves downward too, and vice versa. You can also use your other hand to stroke the exposed base of the penis or use mild sensuous finger movements over the testicles and anal opening. The pace at which you move up and down is a matter of *his* personal preference. Ask him. He'll appreciate your sensitivity to him.

If you are in a position to see, you'll find that after

a few minutes of this kind of intense stimulation the scrotum will begin to tighten and ascend toward the body. This change means that orgasm is imminent. If you're not in a position to see, you'll probably know by his sighs or moans or the tightening of his leg muscles and toes. You can stop, switch to other pleasures, or go on to a climax.

After he climaxes, either of you can take off the condom. Roll it down the penis and lightly pull it off, being careful to keep the ejaculate inside the reservoir at the top. Semen can remain on the penis, so it's a good idea to suggest washing. One woman does this by offering to bathe her lover's penis with a warm steamy washcloth that she brings to bed on a tray with a cool drink and a candle. Do not begin oral sex again unless you use a fresh condom.

If you decide to go on immediately to intercourse and he has not ejaculated, he can keep the condom you've used for oral sex on, but it's preferable to use a fresh one lubricated with nonoxynol-9. In either case, you need to apply nonoxynol-9 lubricant to the outside of the condom and your vaginal lining. The CDC now advises this method as a way of creating a "chemical condom," a double barrier, in order to help prevent transmission of HIV through mucous membranes if semen leaks from the latex.

Several women I talked with said they let a man penetrate the vagina but didn't ask him to put on a condom until just before ejaculation, and the same with oral sex. This is definitely not safe. A team of researchers at Harvard has uncovered new evidence that HIV is present in the fluid that precedes ejaculation. Put a condom on before any intimate contact takes place.

Technique is important, but the most significant aspect of oral sex is simply giving pleasure to your partner. "Any woman can learn to do it," said one man, "but what really counts is when a woman gives me the feeling that she is into what she's doing—and she's doing it for *me*."

eight

Inside the Male Mind

M en," says my closest female friend, who is fond of F. Scott Fitzgerald, "are very different from you and me." Indeed, in the Eighties a great deal of ink was spilled on the dissimilarities between the sexes. Even though you may think you've had enough insight into the male mind, here are some new thoughts from men that I interviewed. I found what they had to say interesting and helpful to women.

Bodies

A thirty-year-old single government employee from Washington, D.C., says, "Physically what attracts me are firm, medium-sized to large breasts, a muscle-toned stomach, lean muscular legs, and tight buns. I guess what all that means is a woman who takes care of herself. I'm also drawn to an attractive face and long hair." After hearing all this I was quite dismayed that a stereotypical body and a pretty face were still foremost in a man's mind. However, he went on, "You know, you say all that and then it turns out to be the personality that actually attracts you. The kind of women who really turn me on are down to earth, funny, intelligent, sensitive, *centered*."

Another man asserted, "Society programs men to turn on to big boobs and they do, but the secondary response is what counts. For me it's a woman who projects confidence that she looks good even when she is not out-and-out beautiful."

"I like all types of bodies," another man claims, "as long as they're fit. I'm also impressed by good posture. It means that a woman feels good about herself. You have to like yourself to be sexy. Self-respect, that's what I go for."

Most of the men I talked with mentioned that they were attracted to women who kept themselves fit. They like a woman who takes care of her body. Details like "clean, shiny hair," "good personal hygiene," "short, polished fingernails," and "natural makeup" were often mentioned as important, but the main message from men: Keep your entire body in good condition. It says you like yourself and it's a turn-on.

What's Sexy

What attracts a man to a woman? When I asked that question ten years ago, the key words were *self-confidence* and *self-assurance*. These are still primary, but another idea is surfacing in the Nineties. In interviewing a thirty-three-year-old doctor about what draws him to certain women, he replied, "Playfulness."

Almost every man I talked with for this book appreciates a woman who approaches life with ease and imagination, a woman who has a sense of humor and isn't too busy to play. I think one reason for that is that while sex makes us vulnerable, in the spontaneity of play we feel free to lower our guards.

The other reason?

Men like variety, the thing they didn't expect.

"Do you know when I really fell in love with my girlfriend?" one man asked me. "The night she suggested that we play hide-and-seek in the dark. Naked. I'd always been wary of settling down. Afraid I'd get bored after a few years. After that night I knew I'd never be bored with her."

Play reminds us that sex isn't a destination. Sex is the journey that takes us there. Men respond to women who make the journey fun.

Here's a story that I found delightful. "Barbara was a blind date," recounted a man from Sante Fe. "I hate blind dates but I kept going on them hoping I'd find someone I wanted to see again. I went to pick up Barbara, rang the bell. She met me at the door of her apartment and before I could even decide what I thought about her, she put her hand on my arm and said, 'Shall we dance?'

" 'Shall We Dance' from *The King and I* was playing on the tape deck. I thought, What the hell, and gave her a whirl around the room. We were both laughing because it was so crazy. The tape ended and she said, 'I hate blind dates. I thought this time, no matter what, I was going to have fun.' Everything she did from there on seemed sexy."

Scents

Smell is the most evocative of our senses; a scent can take us back in time to an almost-forgotten memory. Why miss a chance to remain in his mind? Most men seem to prefer a woman who wears fragrance. But remember they like being tantalized not asphyxiated. To find the scent that will mark you in his memory, try several. When he comments on one, use it often—so it reminds him of you.

A friend of mine recounts the first time he spent in his girlfriend's bed: "The room smelled slightly spicy—of cinnamon and oranges, I think, and the pillowcases smelled like her. It was not overpowering.

All I can remember is something lingering in the air, a scent I'll never forget."

Perfuming the environment is a favorite seduction ploy of the courtesan, and one that a sophisticated woman can make use of. As a matter of fact, aromatherapy, the art of using scent to change or enhance mood, is a hot topic in both scientific and cosmetic journals right now. You might want to dab some essential oils on yourself or your pillows to heighten an erotic experience. The combination of a dim, romantic light and that evocative scent has led more than one man to love. Napoleon was unable to resist Josephine, who always carried a handkerchief saturated with musk. Was he thinking of that alluring scent when he wrote, "A kiss on your heart, and then one a little lower down, much lower down"?

One last word about personal scent. Many men told me that they like a woman who smells "clean." Women who use a diaphragm should be careful that the diaphragm itself doesn't develop an unpleasant odor, which it may do if it is left in place longer than the required six hours.

Good hygiene is clearly a prerequisite for making love. If you're uncomfortable about the scent of your genital area, one therapist recommends tasting your body's natural lubricants in order to experience what your partner tastes.

The easiest way to find out if odor is a problem is to ask. A man might be reluctant to question faulty hygiene, but he should be willing to be honest if you

pose it as a question of health. Say that you read recently that genital odor may indicate a health problem.
Tell him that you would appreciate his letting you
know if any unpleasant odor develops so that you can
make an appointment for a checkup.

Although many women worry about the odor and
taste of vaginal secretions, it should be comforting to
know that none of the men I spoke with had anything
other than positive things to say about taste.

Is Nighttime the Right Time?

Many men will tell you there's a difference between
morning sex and before-bed sex. "Morning sex is an
energizer, a pep talk for my body," says one man.
Others agree: "I like to get it on in the morning because I'm fresh and the night has erased a lot of my
tension." Another reports, "We can be more romantic in the morning because there's less to distract us.
The kids are watching TV, the phone's not ringing,
the beeper isn't on yet."

One physiological reason for these reactions is that
for most men, the level of testosterone (the sex hor-
mone secreted by the testes) is at a high point around
six A.M. It's easier to have and maintain an erection in
the early hours.

Nighttime sex seems to have a slightly different aspect, according to men I talked with. "Sex late at
night tends to be more romantic, to take more time,
to have a more experimental, more unpredictable side

to it," says a forty-four-year-old man who is a neighbor of mine. His girlfriend adds, "If you're in love, sex is great at all times. But if you drink too much, sex becomes mechanical or it sometimes doesn't happen at all. You start to kiss and it seems easier to fall asleep."

(A word here about alcohol and marijuana: Yes, in moderate amounts they can ease anxieties and inhibitions, but any more than restrained use will backfire, as erection difficulties are more likely and drowsiness will almost certainly ensue.)

Men also talked about bad timing. "When I'm going out to play golf, or when I have an important business deal the next day, I'm not that interested in making love," one man told me. "My wife is terrific because she knows exactly when *not* to want sex with me." "If I'm watching Monday-night football, I don't want to be interrupted for romantic stuff," another man stated. "However, I wouldn't say no to my girlfriend giving me head at halftime."

And speaking of halftime, an interesting point: A *Playboy* magazine poll conducted by the Roper Organization in the spring of 1992 revealed that a majority of men, when asked what they considered manly, replied (1) a strong sex drive and (2) sports. This isn't a new message, but it's useful to be reminded that a great many men's minds operate in this way.

Naked or Not

"My wife went on an exercise and diet program," one man recounted, "and for the first time in years she takes off her nightgown when we make love and she keeps the lights on. It really makes a difference for me. It's a big turn-on."

Do men like their women under wraps?

Yes and no.

Men are aroused by the sight of a nude female body. "The first night with a woman is, of course, big on anticipation," says one man. "I'm waiting to see what she looks like without her clothes on. I'm not looking for a perfect body or even great tits, I'm turned on by the idea of nakedness in a woman." Many men concur with this.

They also point out that sexy underwear is a time-tested stimulant. What is it about lacy lingerie that is so appealing? "My theory is that it's the novelty and unpredictability of it," explains a man who buys his girlfriend a sexy thong every few months to ensure his hypothesis. "When you get to see skin that's covered by something sexy like a push-up bra or a bikini, it gives a boost to the hormones," says a thirty-seven-year-old computer whiz. "You imagine what's directly underneath and how soon you can get it off her body."

Body image for women is a very big issue today. Many of us are still uncomfortable with our bodies. We worry that our breasts are too small and our thighs and stomachs too big, that we're not toned and fit enough to be desirable. Keep in mind that the man you're making love to wouldn't be with you if he didn't find you sexually appealing. Even more important than what *he* thinks is how you see yourself. If you believe that you're fit and healthy, that you're in control of your body and how you look, you're going to feel—and be—much sexier. In the Eighties too many women relentlessly worked out in order to achieve an impossible goal, "the perfect body." Nineties thinking is far more sane: A healthy body is a sexy body.

Your Touch

When I wrote *How to Make Love to a Man*, men told me that women's sense of sexual touch was "too timid," "too hesitant," "too feathery," "wavering." Today, men admit that women have grown much more sophisticated in their knowledge of men's bodies, but "grabbiness" is still a problem and a major turn-off.

"I've had it happen to me—a woman has grabbed for my crotch rather than gradually working her way toward it. How would you like it if I zeroed in and seized your breast?" one man inquired. "I've had a woman suddenly stick a pointed tongue down my ear," says another. "It was terrible. No subtlety about it."

"*Do not touch him the way you want to be touched.*" A

man I interviewed dubbed this the Golden Rule of making love. Many of us were taught to please a partner by doing to him what feels good to us. Remember: Men's bodies and musculature are very different from women's. A woman might like the softest of touches, but a man usually prefers a firmer one. You might want the most exquisitely gentle stroking of your clitoris, but most men say they favor a firmer touch on the penis. "The kind of pressure you have when you're holding a tennis racquet" was one man's description.

The majority of men I talked with say that firm is better than feathery. Best of all is the woman who has "a self-assured touch, who projects that she knows what she is doing—and she enjoys doing it," claims a colleague of mine.

The only way to find out what feels best to a man is to experiment and to ask questions about his preferences. When asked "What feels good?" the immediate answer of many men is "Everything." By asking him "How does this feel?" when you're actually touching him, so he can respond to you with *"That* does," you'll identify specifically the areas and pressure that he most responds to.

Your Orgasms

"Knowing that a woman is deeply aroused and has had an earth-shattering orgasm turns me on more than anything else," said one man. "You don't always know when women are faking it, but when you know they *aren't*, that they've really surrendered to the moment and are over the edge—that's a home run." Most men I've talked with would agree with that declaration.

The fact is, however, many women feel they must "reward" their lovers with an orgasm even if it's not a real one. And as anyone who saw Billy Crystal and Meg Ryan in *When Harry Met Sally* knows, faking is not that difficult a feat to accomplish. Many of us have been taught that the be-all and end-all of sex is a thundering climax or multiples thereof and that those orgasms are a sign to a lover that he's pleasured you. We aim to satisfy and please, so we say thank you by faking.

This is not a good practice. Faking orgasm is almost always counterproductive to good or great sex because you can never find out what will make you have a climax and your man can never really know what will give you pleasure. Once you give up performing and concentrate on sensation, you may find that you have the real thing more often.

"I used to fake," one woman told me, "and then I realized that it distanced me from my husband. Now if I don't have one, I might say, 'Honey, that was really fabulous, I didn't have an orgasm—I've had enough good love from you to last a lifetime, so I didn't need one tonight.' "

Most of the advice you'll get about faking is: DON'T. And it's good counsel. But be easy on yourself. If once in a great while, like Meg Ryan, you put on a good show, there's no major harm done. If it's more than every so often, then you're doing him, yourself, and the relationship a disservice. Faking it has no room in true intimacy, which is based on honesty and trust.

His Erection Problems

No man can will an erection. Any man, no matter how young or how old and no matter what he tells you, can have anxiety about sexual "performance." Today, most women recognize that it's not their fault if a lover fails to have an erection. The counsel we've been given over the last decade is to tell him it doesn't matter, there's always a next time. Whatever you say, we're told, don't make him feel as if he's failed. This is good advice as far as it goes. But all those soothing phrases are aimed at reassuring the male. What if they don't work? What if he's impotent the "next time" and the time after? The woman is very often left thinking that she wasn't sexy enough to excite him. She begins to believe the old saw: There are not impotent men, only incompetent women. Is that true? No, it is not.

It's estimated that more than 30 million American men of all ages suffer from impotence. Current figures indicate that in 75 to 80 percent of the cases, the cause is physical, not psychological.

Fatigue and tension may originate in the mind, but

they cause differences in the ways that the body functions. Even if we were to discount the psychological conditions brought on by lifestyle, there are other physical causes of impotence: side effects from certain common prescription drugs (for hypertension and migraine, for example), high cholesterol, insufficient amounts of testosterone, alcohol, and recreational drugs.

If your lover has erection problems that last over six weeks, you should stop thinking of it as a temporary condition. Encourage him to have a checkup and discuss the problem with a doctor. Impotence is very often a symptom of an underlying health problem. And it can be cured. There are many techniques that have been developed over the last decade that restore potency. A good urologist should be up to date on the subject. Or you can call the Impotence Institute of America, which operates a hot line that answers questions on impotence and provides information on what help is available (Impotence Anonymous Hotline, 1-800-669-1603).

(nine)

Sexy
New
Sex
Techniques

Years ago when sex researchers Masters and Johnson confirmed that women could have multiple
orgasms, a media frenzy ensued. Every women's magazine and most TV talk shows featured pieces on sex
and orgasm. For many women, the "capacity for"
translated into "obligation to." The emphasis on peak
performance put unnecessary pressure on men and
women alike. Men had to perform, while women felt
compelled to "orgasm" in order not to disappoint
their hardworking partners.

Let's keep the mechanical aspects of sex in perspective. *Satisfaction*, not orgasm, is what counts with most women—and there are numerous studies to prove it. As we get further into the Nineties, *satisfaction* and *prolonged pleasure* will be key words for men too. There are myriad ways to feel deeply, erotically, sensually, and sexually satisfied besides the big O. The healthy attitude that's surfaced in the last five years is *More is not necessarily better*, and we shouldn't forget it.

In the next pages you'll be reading about the news in sexuality. There is the Coital Alignment Technique (CAT), Non-Ejaculatory Male Orgasms (NEMOs), and U spots. I've also included some ancient love techniques that haven't been yet been popularized. Even though you can have fabulous orgasm(s) with all of them, these innovations don't *require* you to have a climax. While it makes good sense to be physiologically and anatomically sensitive to each other, it doesn't mean you have to go overboard with sexual mechanics. Read the following pages and focus on pleasure, satisfaction—and fun!

The CAT

When a book promising to reveal this new secret for great sex came across my desk, I gave it my immediate attention. Written by Edward Eichel and Philip Nobile, the book is entitled *The Perfect Fit: How to Achieve Mutual Fulfillment and Monogamous Passion Through the New Intercourse*.

We ran instructions for this "new intercourse" in

Self magazine and also asked two couples to write up their personal experiences with the CAT, following Eichel and Nobile's rules. After the article appeared many readers wrote to say that they were ecstatic at finding a technique that gave them such great sex—in the missionary position, no less.

Other readers wrote to say that they'd been stroking the CAT all along. "We've been doing your position for years," wrote a woman from Ohio, "only we didn't know it had a name. It's the best kind of sex. I get really deep orgasms every time."

The authors of the CAT claimed that the technique made orgasm a sure thing for women: 77 percent of Eichel's female subjects climaxed "always or almost always" using it. In addition, "The alignment intensified orgasm in 71 percent of males and 45.5 percent of the females," writes Eichel's coauthor, Philip Nobile.

The only problem that some couples have found with the CAT is that it takes patience and practice. It involves motions that are contrary to the ones we usually associate with making love, and if habit makes you rush toward orgasm, this technique is not going to work for you. The key to mastering the CAT is your ability to communicate with your partner and to work together to learn the movements.

Here, for you, are the instructions:

1. *The Start.* The authors explain that "partners begin the CAT by assuming the usual missionary position." The man lies on top with his legs be-

tween her legs. He inserts his penis but does not let his weight rest on top of her, resting instead on his elbows.

2. *The Fit.* Next, the man slides toward his partner's head into what the authors call the "riding high" position. In this manner, the authors explain, "the base of his penis is brought into direct contact with her clitoris."

Now the man lets his chest rest against his partner's, moving slightly to the side to achieve a comfortable position but making sure that his pelvis lies a bit above his partner's. This position, which the authors refer to as a "small but significant adjustment," is crucial to the CAT. To keep the man from sliding down into a more accustomed position, the woman wraps her legs around him. She should not raise her legs or spread her knees, but keep her body aligned with her lover's.

The point of the CAT is to establish a rhythm that is as interdependent as a seesaw. The movement of one partner depends on the movement of the other. That is why the position is so important. To keep the movements connected, the partners' bodies must remain in tight contact.

3. *The Stroke.* The CAT rhythm is a coordinated upward and downward stroke, the movement measured and steady. Instead of pulling apart and thrusting together, the stroke of the penis travels

about two inches, and partners at all time maintain *full body contact*. The woman leads by pressing upward; he gently resists, but this is *"resistance without force,"* a motion that is more a rocking together than a thrusting against. On the downward stroke, the pattern is reversed, with the man exerting just enough pressure to affect a shallow entry, and the woman offering just enough resistance to maintain total genital contact. The rhythm in the two pubic areas allows for a natural friction between the genitals.

4. *Genital Contact and Orgasm* The CAT's genital "circuitry" is complete, the authors explain, "when the penis is in the vagina and in contact with the clitoris at the same time." The rhythm must be steady. The authors caution, "Partners must try to avoid the archetypal—almost reflexive—tendency to speed up and 'grasp' at orgasm. . . ." Rhythm and contact are maintained by a slow, rocking motion. Each stroke should last at least several seconds. In speeding up, the man pulls too far back and, in trying for a deeper thrust, breaks contact with the clitoris. Remember that it is the steady, rhythmic rocking of the penis in the vagina, with the top of the penis stimulating the clitoris, that leads to orgasm.

Learning the CAT takes patience, and some couples trying it for the first time find that the man loses his erection. If this occurs, a momentary return to the more familiar pattern of deep thrusts will usually restore it. Then the couple can slide back into the CAT position and the slower, rocking rhythm. When the alignment goes completely awry, it is usually because the man becomes impatient or fearful of losing his erection. He then abandons the CAT and reverts to traditional thrusting. Sometimes it is the woman who breaks the rhythm by slowing down or stopping.

"The point to reread," writes Karen E. Bender in her appraisal of the CAT for *Self*, "is the 'small but significant' adjustment described in Step 2. . . . The movements are controlled and delicate, the erotic equivalent of a Monet."

NEMOs

Only in the last few years has the sexology community acknowledged that the phenomenon of male multiple orgasms does indeed exist. Sex researcher William Masters has maintained that in the his thirty-five years of research he's found only two males with the m.o. capability, but some men have long insisted that they *can* have several orgasms and now research is backing them up.

William Hartman, Ph.D., former president of the Society for the Scientific Study of Sex, and his colleague Marilyn Fithian wrote *Any Man Can* (1984), which documents their research on male multiple orgasms and also explains the techniques a man can use to experience them.

The pair did their studies on an intriguing machine called the dynograph recorder, which measures a variety of functions: blood flow, heart rate, contractions of the pelvic and anal muscles, and more. Using this device, the two researchers studied orgasm in 282 male and 469 female volunteers. Their scientific conclusion: Some males turned out to be capable of multiple orgasms, averaging two or three orgasms before ejaculation. Many of these men had the capability naturally, while others had trained themselves to rise to the challenge.

A large number of women, about 75 percent according to Hartman, achieved multiple orgasms. Even more, according to Masters, have a natural capacity for m.o.'s, but not all want to have them and some have never experienced them.

In *The Male Sexual Machine* (1992) by Kenneth Purvis, M.D., Ph.D., a researcher in male sexuality at the National Hospital in Oslo, Norway, writes of studies that have discovered men who can have three to ten orgasms before ejaculation—and one man who had thirty orgasms in an hour!

The news that multiple orgasms are not limited to women may have come as a surprise to sex researchers, but many a wife has known it for some time. One woman wrote to tell me about her husband's ability to have several orgasms before ejaculation.

"He does admit it is a 'tightrope act,' " she says, "but if the timing is right, he can do this more than once. Don't tell him he's special. It might go to his head."

But is he special? A little, since he seems to be one of the men who achieve NEMOs (Non-Ejaculatory Male Orgasms) naturally.

Experiencing NEMOs is like poising on the end of a diving board, as one man described it. Each time you bounce a little higher, but you don't dive into the water. You keep in control. Then, finally, you let yourself go, floating higher and higher until gravity takes over and you plunge fast and hard into a deep dark sea.

For this man, the mini-orgasms that precede ejaculation intensify the final one, bringing him closer and closer to the edge before he finally lets go.

A few men say that though they, too, are able to have several orgasms before ejaculation, each of the orgasms, including the final one, is somewhat less intense than it would be if they had only one. "It depends on how I feel," explains one man. "Sometimes I find it more exciting to prolong the pleasure, even if the final orgasm isn't quite as strong."

If the man in your life is not among the lucky few who were born doing a balancing act, there is a way he can teach himself the technique. The trick lies in learning how to reach the point of ejaculation and then to pull back, maintaining the erection. That is the key to NEMOs: the ability to separate orgasm and ejaculation and feel them as two distinctly different sensations. Hartman claims that he has never encountered a man who tried to learn NEMOs and couldn't. He and Fithian detail the strategy in *Any Man Can*, and here, in abbreviated form, it is:

Step 1: Ejaculatory Control. Once you learn to control ejaculation you're on your way to experiencing NEMOs. Some men can stop ejaculation simply by withdrawing from the vagina for several seconds. If that doesn't work, there are three other ways to stop. Either you or your lover can squeeze the penis, applying pressure to the slightly rounded ridge on the underside of the penis, or you can use your fingers to prevent his testicles from rising. As the testicles begin to ascend toward the body, very gently push them down. Both of these techniques are usually enough to stop ejaculation and either of you can use them.

The third way to control ejaculation involves tightening of the PC, or pubococcygeus muscle. This is a variation of the exercises most women know as the Kegels, which are prescribed for helping childbirth and also for experiencing multiple orgasms more easily.

This is how PC exercises work for men.

First, the man locates the PC muscle. It's the same one used to stop urine flow midstream. After locating it, he simply contracts the muscle (as he would to stop urination) and holds it contracted for ten to fifteen seconds. He repeats this ten times. He contracts the muscle again but lets go almost immediately and repeats this "flick" ten times.

The goal: To work up to one hundred each of the flicks per day plus two or three of the extended contractions, or Rolls-Royces, as Hartman has dubbed them. Over eight to twelve weeks, a man can gain control of the PC muscle and it should be strong enough for ejaculatory control.

Step 2: Finding "the Cliff." Once the PC is strengthened, the man needs to locate his own "point of no return," known in sexology parlance as "ejaculatory inevitability." At the moment when a man feels that he is going to ejaculate (this has been described as being akin to the start of a sneeze!), he uses one of the methods above—that is, withdrawal, squeezing the penis, pushing down the testicles, and/or squeezing his PC muscle. He will experience an orgasm without ejaculation (a.k.a. NEMO) and can then go on thrusting until another point of no return is reached. The men whom I interviewed who have experienced NEMOs say that they can repeat this pattern three to five times. Most report a final orgasm complete with ejaculation as "incredibly intense."

"Some men have the ability to time their ejaculation down to the actual thrust," one doctor explained to me. "This kind of refined awareness takes time and acute sensitivity to the threshold of ejaculation." It takes practice to get this kind of control, but given American's mania for working out, it wouldn't sur-

prise me if a good number of men don't start strength-
ening those PC muscles right away.

The U Spot

Recently Kevin E. McKenna, Ph.D., an associate pro-
fessor of physiology at Northwestern University Medical School, and his colleagues found out an
extraordinary thing about laboratory rats. As reported
in 1988 in *Neuroscience Letters*, the researchers said,
"the coitus reflex [orgasm] can be reliably and repeat-
edly elicited in both male and female rats by mechanical stimulation of the urethra."

What does this mean for humans? Lab rats resemble
humans in their sexual anatomy, and thus a new era
of orgasms may be dawning in the Nineties.

The most recent research from the McKenna group
found that serotonin, a neurotransmitter produced by
cells in the urethra, brain, and elsewhere in the body,
and which is thought to be involved with controlling
states of consciousness and mood, enhances the ability
of lab rats to have orgasms. Dr. McKenna believes
that "the key to female orgasm resides not in the vagina or clitoris but in the urethra." And thus the U
spot orgasm was coined.

You may remember the G spot. In 1982, Alice
Ladas, Beverly Whipple, and John Perry published
The G Spot, in which they discussed a spot on the
upper or anterior side of the vagina that, when stimulated, gave women exceedingly intense orgasms. Al-

though many women say they have not been able to locate it, the existence of the G spot is fairly well accepted among sexologists today. The Northwestern researchers believe that there may be a connection between the so-called U spot and the elusive G spot.

You don't have to wait until you hear about their conclusions, however, to do some experimenting on your own, or with your partner. The urethral canal is embedded in the front wall of the vagina, with its tiny orifice directly in front of the vaginal opening and about an inch behind the clitoris. Check out an anatomy book if you need further directions.

Try stimulating the small surface area around the urethal opening with your fingers. You can do this during intercourse or have your lover do this when he is stimulating you manually on the clitoris.

Some women claim that there is more sensation in the area when the bladder is full. This makes sense. If the bladder is distended, there's more area to stimulate and more sensation to feel. Some women also report that medium pressure applied with the heel of the hand to the spot just above the pubic bone (about three to four inches beneath the navel in most women) when they are being stimulated manually also greatly enhances orgasm. This may—or may not—be a function of the U spot. It will be up to the Northwestern researchers to let us know.

A Thousand Strokes

Sexuality in Western civilization has had its ups and downs, but in the East sex was always a spiritual as well as a physical union. Sex was natural, sex was communion, sex was sexy. Almost two thousand years ago both the *Tao* of China and *The Kama Sutra* of India were instructing men and women in techniques and postures which were as erotic as anything you'll find in today's most graphic sex manuals.

The Taoists believed that life must be lived in harmony with nature. If a man wanted to reach enlightenment, he must be careful not to waste his essence. Women, they believed, were closer to nature than men, and a man's chance of reaching the higher plane increased if he could gather a woman's essence and add it to his own.

How did they go about this?

By bringing the woman to frequent orgasm, thus capturing her juices. For a look at the variety and inventiveness that those erotic ancients brought to sexual union, you have only to glance through *The Tao of Sex* (1989) by Howard S. Levy and Akira Ishihara.

"When having intercourse for the first time," the authors translate from the ancient text, "a man arranges the woman on her back and kneels between her thighs." Inserting his penis, he then presses in and out while fondling her clitoris.

"He kisses her mouth and sucks her tongue." Then, as the woman's vaginal area grows moist, he carries out the "nine shallow, one deep" technique, pushing only the head of his penis into the vagina, and continuing this shallow penetration for nine strokes before, on the tenth stroke, he enters with a deep, powerful thrust.

He "leans vertically and loiters horizontally, pulling nearby and drawing out alongside. Sometimes he is leisurely or quick, at other times he is deep or shallow. . . . [He] rapidly inserts and quickly pierces; he pierces in and out, elevating his waist. He awaits the woman's agitation and adapts the slowness and quickness [of his movements] accordingly."

Note the way the man is guided in his thrusting by the woman's response. To achieve the ultimate sexual satisfaction, it was not just the position that mattered, but how deeply and how often a man entered his mate. The repeated shallow penetrations recommended by the *Tao* are highly arousing, heightening the stimulation of both the clitoris and the glans of the penis.

How many strokes should a man make? The *Tao* tells us that as well. (The "jade stalk" if you can't figure it out, is the penis.)

"Have the woman face downwards in a crawling position, buttocks up and head down. The male kneels behind her and embraces her belly. Then he inserts the jade stalk and stabs it exceedingly within her. He strives to make it deeply intimate. They go back and forth in mutual pressure; if carried out to the numbers of five and eight, the [proper] degree is naturally obtained. The woman's vagina is closed and extended, and when her emission fluid overflows outwards, [the intercourse] is ended and you rest."

In this position, the man penetrates deeply into his lover's vagina, and she, in turn, presses back up against him, making his penis slide even further inside her. He enters rapidly and shallowly five times and then pulls back and reenters her with eight driving motions, rocking back and forth, stimulating the walls of the vagina, rubbing and reaching into the very depths of her.

In another position (there are thirty, plus variations), the man sits straight up on the bed, his legs extended in front of him, while the woman kneels over his penis, her back to him. She holds his penis in her hand and lowers herself onto it. Once he is inside her, he holds her around the waist and thrusts deeply in and out.

Because she is kneeling, the woman is able to raise and lower herself, making it easier for him to penetrate. The position also helps her to control the motion in ways that will give her the most pleasure. Women who have tried it say that it is particularly good in stimulating the G spot.

"Superlatively excellent," says the text, now showing a man and woman standing. The woman leans against him, her back resting against his chest. She then bends forward, until her hands touch the floor, or, if she's not sufficiently supple, she rests on a chair, a stool, or a stack of pillows. The man clasps her around the waist and thrusts in from behind, with the angle of her body again making it possible for him to penetrate deeply. And again stimulating the G spot.

None of these positions and movements is designed simply for male pleasure. The man is withholding his own ejaculation in order to stimulate the woman.

To help your lover learn control, you might suggest that the two of you practice the Set of Nines. In this exercise the man enters the woman with nine shallow thrusts. He withdraws and pauses before entering again, thrusting shallowly and quickly for eight times and then pushing inside for one, last, deep thrust.

Again he withdraws, pulling back briefly from the edge of orgasm before entering again. (You can also help him control ejaculation by using the "Western" techniques outlined on pages 105–107). Now he takes seven shallow strokes, just allowing the head of his penis to penetrate the vagina, before finishing the motion with two deep thrusts. The Set of Nines continues—six shallow, three deep, five shallow, four deep—until the man brings his lover to orgasm with nine deep, thrusting strokes.

Those who practice the Tao of sex claim that a man who has trained himself in these methods can bring a woman to incredible orgasm by entering her with a thousand strokes.

"If you're willing to train for golf, tennis, or running, why not for love?" says an expert, Richard M. Chin, M.D., of the East West Institute and the Acupuncture and Qi Kung Manipulative Therapy Center

in New York City. "If you think of the act of love as
an art form—a kind of cosmic dance of awareness in
which every nuance of your lover's body is important—you'll realize it's not ejaculation that provides
fulfillment, but all that leads up to it. Be aware of sub-
tleties of smell, taste, touch. The sound of a sigh . . .
One must be able to go far beyond the Western con-
cept of orgasms."

Tantric Yoga

The practice of Tantric yoga lets us bring an intensity
of concentration to sex. In India, the Tantric religion,
devoted to worship of the mother goddess, focuses on
female energy and teaches that sexual union can
become a way of communing with the gods.

I knew a bit about yoga but was not familiar with
Tantric yoga until one of the editors of *Self* and her
husband went on a retreat in California where the
techniques were taught. She came back so enthusiastic
about the experience that I decided to do some research on it. Modern practitioners of Tantric Yoga
recommend exercises that can teach couples to merge
their sexual energy. Making love is not two people
taking separate satisfactions but a union where the
boundaries of the bodies are dissolved and two people
become one.

To understand the ways of Tantric yoga, get a
copy of *Jewel in the Lotus: The Sexual Path to Higher
Consciousness,* by Sunyata Saraswati and Bodhi

Avinasha, or *Tantra: The Yoga of Sex* (1983), by Omar Garrison.

In the meantime, here are several exercises you might find interesting:

The man lies next to the woman, who is on her back. He is to the right of her, reclining on his left side and facing her. The woman bends her knees and draws them up against her chest. The man then swings the top of his body away from her, bringing his penis into contact with her genitals. The woman straightens her legs, capturing the man's right leg between her legs. When this is done properly, it brings the sexual organs of the partners into close contact that can be prolonged without tension or discomfort.

When they are fully relaxed, the man parts the woman's labia with his fingers and partially inserts his penis. At this point he does *not* penetrate deeply. The point of the exercise is contact, not intercourse.

In this position, the partners lie motionless for thirty-two minutes, visualizing the flow of energy between them, concentrating on the sexual contact in a way that Garrison describes as "not forced or tense, but performed in a detached almost somnolent way."

What is the point of all this? Western students of Tantra say that somewhere between the twenty-eighth and thirty-second minute of contact, you will experience an abrupt excitement, causing involuntary contractions of the entire body—not just a sexual orgasm but one that can shake your entire being.

Here's another experience that Tantric yoga describes as a "meditation." It is designed to increase the flow of energy between the man and the woman. It may or may not lead to intercourse, but it definitely will make you feel closer to your lover.

Lie together on your left sides, nestling into each other spoon fashion. Close your eyes and begin to breathe together. Inhale, hold your breath, exhale. Try it for five to ten minutes and you'll see how it intensifies your awareness of your partner, how the effort of joining your breath both relaxes and arouses.

In another meditation, The Thunderbolt, you kneel facing each other, knees touching. Sit back on your heels. First, raise your hands to shoulder height and press your palms into his. Each of you gazes steadily into each other's left eye. This may sound odd, but it's much easier to stare into one of your partner's eyes than to try to focus on both. Eyes locked, palms pressed together, slowly inhale. Tighten your pelvic muscles and lift your joined hands overhead while rising up on your knees. Then, as you exhale, reverse the process, lowering your hands to shoulder level, and again sit on your heels. Repeat the cycle, rising as you inhale, settling back as you exhale, gazes locked, hands touching, for three to five minutes. Then slide together to the floor and lie in each other's arms.

Tantric yoga not only increases awareness before intercourse, it prolongs the time of union. After the Tantric rituals have led you to intercourse, climax can be postponed through the Tantric Kiss.

Just before you reach orgasm, sit on his lap with his

penis still inside you and your legs wrapped around
each other. You both should remain perfectly still,
pressing your foreheads together and letting the breath
of one flow into the body of the other. Your partner
exhales as you inhale. As you expel your breath, he
inhales it. The energy of one becomes the energy of
the other. The soul of one flows into the body of the
other. Even couples just learning Tantric yoga are
urged to prolong the Tantric Kiss for at least ten minutes. I was fervently assured by the *Self* editor who
experienced The Kiss that the orgasm that follows is
"cosmic."

ten

Talk
It
to Me

When you talk about sex, you ruin it," said a
man who believes in the swept-away school of
romance. Love is mystical, he insists: You *know* what
the other one wants.

Many of us believe that love has a language of its
own. But no matter how much you love someone,
you don't automatically know his tastes. You have to
learn them. That takes time and it takes talk.

"I don't feel comfortable telling my boyfriend
where I'd like him to touch me," said a twenty-nine-
year-old woman, "so I try to let him know by my
reactions."

Of course, there are nonverbal methods to communicate information about what you want or don't want—a soft sigh when he's caressing you in just the way you like, a sudden change of position to let him know that pleasure has edged into pain. It works. Sort of. Your partner will get the general idea, but he won't get a hint of the other places where his touch could please.

Whether you want to know your partner's favorite color, the sexual positions that excite him, or his sexual history, you must learn to ask. You're going to have to inform, discuss, suggest, advise, enlighten—in a word, *talk*—with each other about what you want and need. Equally important is learning to listen.

Communication has always been necessary to keep love alive; in the era of AIDS, it's necessary to keep *us* alive. The confidence we need to discuss condoms, HIV tests, and the crucial issue of fidelity will also teach us to ask for the things that please us.

What's so terrible about asking a man if he's ever looked back on an affair and regretted it because the woman might have put him at risk? What's so bad about saying to a man that tonight, instead of climbing into bed in your flannel nightie, you'd like to make love leaning up against a wall wearing nothing but a garter belt.

I'm aware that it's not so easy to talk about these matters. After I wrote *How to Make Love to a Man*, I was told that, to help promote the book, I was expected to appear on television.

I was aghast—and a wreck. I could *write* about sex, but *talk* about it? On national *television?* The publishers were wise enough to send me to a media specialist, who helped me through the trauma. She asked me how I interviewed men on sex. How, specifically, did I *talk* face-to-face with a man about his most intimate thoughts and experiences?

"Very matter-of-factly," I told her. After my first several interviews I realized the only way to communicate with men (or women) about sex was to sound comfortable, relaxed, and totally nonjudgmental.

She advised me to follow the same standard whenever I discussed my work or my book on radio and television.

Her counsel helped in my personal life as well. I found that I could talk about very sensitive issues with the man who was dearest to me if I appeared self-confident, comfortable, relaxed—even when I wasn't. The effect on him was to make him feel less awkward and more at ease himself.

Why is it so difficult to talk about intimate matters? Because you risk so much. You expose your deepest self in sex. In asking or telling, you risk ridicule and, most frightening, you risk rejection. But if you want the best sexual relationship, you must take those risks.

In her fine, best-selling book, *You Just Don't Understand*, Deborah Tannen uses the word *genderlect* to indicate the differences between the ways men and women communicate with each other. The gridlock between the sexes that many of us feel is situated in these divergent communication styles. "Understanding the other's ways of talking," she writes, "is a giant leap across the communication gap between men and women, and a giant step toward opening lines of communication." And, I might add, a giant help in making love.

I believe that talking about sex or acknowledging that a "problem" might exist is, for many men, an admission of *failure* and requires too much risk so they clam up. Women tend to see a conversation as a comfort and as the beginning of a resolution. On the other hand, we often avoid talking about sex because we're afraid of "hurting a man's feelings" or being considered "too aggressive." Translate the latter to "nonfeminine, nondesirable."

Many women I interviewed admitted that they would rather be sexually uncomfortable than risk the rejection they might face if they owned up to their sexual desires. "My husband just doesn't take the time I need. I've always praised his prowess as a lover. Am I going to do a turnaround now and tell him he's less than terrific? No way. I wouldn't want to risk my marriage," says one forthright woman who's settling for a lot less than she should.

"I'd like to let my boyfriend know that there are other things we could be doing, but he's less experienced than I am," admits one woman. "How should I tell him without sounding like I've been sleeping around a lot—which I haven't."

Before you say one word to your lover, have a conversation with yourself. Ask yourself: *What do I really want? Do I know what he really wants?* Once you've taken stock of where you stand, have the confidence to accept your own desires and to find out his.

When you're talking about sex, therapists advise that you talk about yourself first. Tell your lover your own needs, wishes, limitations, hang-ups. Then ask him to tell you what he thinks about what you've said. The point is to have an *exchange* of information between the two of you that leads to a clearer understanding of what you both want.

Talk between lovers should be absolutely clear. Be specific: "I'd love you to do that" or "It feels a little too rough there" or "I'm worried that I don't know how to do oral sex the right way."

Once you've talked, then you need to listen. According to communications experts, most of us listen at about 25 percent efficiency. The idea is that you have something to *learn* from what the other person is saying. "Your attitude is so important when you talk about sex," says a New York marriage counselor. "Keep your mind open. So many people tune out because they're afraid of hearing something that will upset them. Most times this is not the case. You're going to benefit from communication."

If, like many of us, you're not yet confident enough to broach a subject with your partner, you might want to try these suggestions:

IF YOU WANT TO KNOW
ABOUT THE OTHER WOMEN IN HIS LIFE

"How many women have you been to bed with?"
"How many did you know well enough to know their
sexual pasts?" You can ask him questions like these
outright, but a shockingly high number of men I
talked with admitted that, if they thought honesty
would hurt the current relationship, they might lie
about past partners.

The best way to handle this is to *assume* a new lover
may be seeing other women. To find out more, you're
going to have to wait a bit.

A friend of mine told me this hilarious story, which
I think is relevant.

"Not long after I met Peter, I knew he was someone
I could really care about. When we began to get seri-
ous, I told him I was worried about AIDS and that
before I went to bed with him I wanted to know his
sexual history. Other women he'd been with.

"He sat down at my desk and started writing. And
writing. And writing. I got more and more upset. Finally I screamed 'Stop!'

"He said, 'But I've only gotten to fifty-seven.' The
relationship would have ended right there except it
finally occurred to me that he was pulling my leg. I
told him, 'Never mind. I assume you aren't the last
male virgin in Manhattan. When we go to bed, we're
going to use a condom.' "

Charlotte's assumption that a new lover probably

has dated other women is, I think, a pragmatic one. Even though you may have sex together early in a relationship, it takes time for two people to make a commitment to each other. Along the way, you'll find many opportunities to ask your lover about his past.

IF YOU'D LIKE HIM TO DO SOMETHING DIFFERENT

You've spent months or years assuring a man your sex life together is fine. Naturally, he's going to be hurt if you suddenly take the initiative in a way that suggests you've never been pleased at all.

This is how Pat did it. She told her husband that he was reaching a dangerous age. The age of The Other Woman. She told him, "I'm going to be your other woman." She began dressing more flamboyantly, bought several erotic books, and in the evening, instead of settling down in front of the TV set, she lit some candles, took out her cache of books, and read passages to her husband. They began trying new things in bed. "Our sex life had been stagnating," she said, "and this 'other woman' approach revved it up big time."

When Tracy asked her boyfriend what sexual positions were best for him, he said they were all good. When she asked him which touch he most enjoyed, he said anything was fine. Tracy decided that if they were going to talk openly about their sexual desires, she'd have to take the lead. One night she told her

boyfriend, "Tonight I'm going to do one thing—
just one—to please you sexually. You choose what
it is."

That evening Tracy learned that he liked a certain
pattern: oral sex and then intercourse when he was
about to have an orgasm. The next night he offered to
do one thing that would please her. She asked him to
run a bath for her and put a glass of wine next to the
bed. "I found out what he wanted," she said, "then I
let him know that I needed more time and more romance before we actually had sex." Both had discovered how much sexier sex is when you get exactly
what you want. Now they ask openly.

IF YOU'D LIKE HIM
TO MAKE LOVE MORE OFTEN

You want to make love but maybe you're sending
mixed messages—snuggling into his lap, licking his
ear, and then saying, "I shouldn't be doing this, we
both have to get up early." This may sound to you
like a question: Is he too tired to make love? What *he*
hears is that you're feeling slightly sexy but would prefer a good night's sleep.

If you want to make love more often, one of the
best ways to deal with the problem is to enlist his
help. Therapists recommend that you use the "I" approach. Instead of saying "You've lost interest," the
better way is to say, "I need some help. I miss making
love. What can we do about it?" This is nonthreaten-

ing and usually leads to a beneficial discussion about how to improve the situation.

IF YOU WANT HIM
TO BE MORE ROMANTIC

If he gave you lacy lingerie and you raced back to the store and exchanged it for gloves, don't ask why he's not romantic. He's not because you're not.

Does a candlelit dinner make him complain that he can't see what he's eating? Romance isn't candlelight; it's the unexpected. When he comes home planning to park himself in front of the TV, pack a picnic and take him to the ballpark.

Romance is about adventures that will please both of you. Here's an example. Recounts a man from Manhattan: "My girlfriend made a date with me to have a 'surprise' lunch. She picked me up at the office, we got into a cab, ended up at the Empire State Building, and took an elevator to the top. We went into the coffee shop there and she pulled a backgammon board out of her bag. We had hamburgers and played three killer games. Any woman who's that much fun is someone I could really commit to. I proposed to her that same night."

Instead of talking about romance, talk about what each of you likes and use that knowledge to create romance. This man's girlfriend knew he was crazy about backgammon and parlayed it into an unexpected event that was fun and romantic.

Another woman I know works a question about a man's favorite music into the conversation on the first date. If she's interested in him, she buys tapes of what he likes and has them playing the next time he walks in the door. After he comments on it, she says, "I'm glad you noticed. I bought them especially for you. A friend once did the same for me. I thought it was so sweet of her. I love it when people do special things for each other." He remembered that she was a choco-holic, and on their next date he brought her a box of Godiva truffles.

A friend of mine was having trouble in her mar-riage. She wanted her husband to be more romantic and to pay more attention to her. Her wise mother-in-law advised her to set the dinner table with flowers every evening. "I'll do it, but he'll never notice," the young woman responded.

The mother took her son aside and suggested that he tell his wife how lovely the flowers were. She also said that his wife was a true romantic and what did he think was romantic? "Champagne, I guess," he said. "And flowers," his mother added.

"Charlie's being so adorable," the daughter re-ported a few weeks later. "He's bringing me cham-pagne and roses. It made me feel so much closer to him that I suggested that we go away for a long romantic weekend. Things have gotten a lot better between us."

WHEN HE/YOU WOULD LIKE
TO TRY A FANTASY

In playing out fantasies—or even in just discussing them—new channels of communication can be opened up between lovers. "As husband and wife," one woman explained, "we can't talk easily about sex, but when we play roles we can tell each other anything."

She gives this example in her marriage: "Don came home from a trip to L.A. with all sorts of underwear from Frederick's of Hollywood. It was a joke but I took the bait and put on the bra that had the nipples cut out, the garter belt, black stockings, the whole bit. I added a pair of high heels and sauntered into the living room looking like what I imagined was a high-class hooker. He got right into it and asked what I charged.

"I told him that if he paid me five dollars he could play with my breasts. Each time he put his hands somewhere else I'd set a new price. By the time we finished I'd lost count of what he owed.

"The experience was fun but there was an added dimension," she continued. "During the whole time we talked about what men wanted from pros and I found out a great deal about him that I'd never known in four years of marriage."

Several men I talked with declared that they would love a woman to suggest new sexual ideas but very few do. One man recommended that a woman say, "What do you want me to do to you tonight?" If the man gives the usual answer, "Everything," tell him, "I want to know specifically—tell me in detail." That's the kind of conversational lead-in that very few men are able to resist, and it can open up exciting new worlds for both partners.

HOW TO SAY NO
WITHOUT HURT FEELINGS

Instead of talking openly we often use codes. Codes let us say no without using the word. The husband who reads until his wife is asleep, the wife who makes a great to-do before bedtime about how very tired she is and how early she has to get up are both sending sexual signals. Instead of discussing sex, they set up a situation that eliminates it.

Some people reject by actions. Others are afraid to reject at all. One woman told me about the first month of her marriage. Her husband had a new job that kept him late each night; she was preparing for a major sales meeting. Yet night after night, as they climbed into bed, he rolled over and caressed her, beginning long, sensual lovemaking.

"We weren't getting to sleep until two in the morning. But I couldn't bring myself to say no. I didn't want him to feel I was rejecting him. Finally, I couldn't take it anymore. As he started to make love to me, I said, 'Would you mind if we didn't tonight? I'm really tired.' And he said, 'Thank God.'

"He thought it was what *I* wanted. That was really a lesson for me in being honest about how I feel."

"I have no problem with saying no," states another woman. "I just say no, but I always add, 'Let's make a date for tomorrow morning, or I want to treat you to a romantic evening on Saturday.' I let him know I still want him."

On these pages I've outlined some simple ways to talk to each other. To make the words work, you need a few more things: willingness, openness, and a loving spirit. Your positive attitude about communication will make it easier for both of you to express all that you want—and to receive it.

eleven

The Beverly Hills Hotel, Room 207

I was waiting for Tom on the sofa outside the Polo Lounge. It was unusual for him to be late, but I was glad to have some moments to think clearly. Our schedules were so crazy that it had taken four months to get together for our seven dates so far. Eight, if you included drinks last night before he went back to his office to brief himself on the trial he was working on.

"I think of myself as a sophisticated, independent woman with a terrific job and wonderful friends, but when it came to Tom, I felt as if I'd regressed to adolescence. In truth I had known him since I was fourteen and our families had been close. His brother and mine had been—and still were—best friends. Tom and I had been pals for years, although we'd never had a boy/girl relationship.

"Since our first real 'date,' I thought about Tom constantly. I replayed conversations we'd had over and over, I found myself daydreaming about asking him to go to the Caribbean for a long weekend, I fantasized about the kind of apartment we could have together. I woke up every morning in a kind of sweet reverie in which he played the leading role.

"But what kind of role did I have in his life? I really didn't know. We hadn't even been to bed together. I would have jumped at the chance, and so, I'm pretty sure, would he. But because I'd been covering the presidential campaign, and he'd been working since the day I met him on this huge precedent-breaking environmental case, we'd never spent more than dinnertime together. He always had to get back to the office or I had to catch a plane. And we'd laughed about it. This is the Nineties, your life is supposed to be more balanced, we commiserated, work is not the whole enchilada.

"My thoughts were interrupted by this fabulous-looking guy with sandy hair falling into his blue eyes, wearing a slightly rumpled gray suit with the tie loosened.

" 'Alice.' " He smiled and leaned down to give me a kiss on the cheek.

"My heart was literally pounding at seeing him.

" 'I'm sorry I'm late. I still don't have the knack of getting around L.A. Subways look much better than Porsches to me these days. I'll be glad to get back to New York next week.'

"He took my arm and led me into the Polo Lounge, saying to the maître d', 'Name's Loew. I made a reservation for two at seven.'

"Something about being in a different city made us closer. We reminisced about our childhoods, our dreams, the romances in our past. We were sitting, legs touching, in a round booth and both of us felt the sexual charge in the air.

" 'I'm going to pay the bill,' he said with a wonderful smile, never taking his eyes off me, 'Why don't you come up to my room? I would really like it if you would.'

" 'Let me have a minute to think,' I replied. I didn't need a millisecond to make the decision, but I wanted at least to appear to hesitate in a nice-girl manner.

"He put his arm around me and kissed the back of my neck. I didn't say a word, stood up, took his hand, and let him lead me.

"I can tell you I have never felt this way. I admit it was lust because I wanted to feel his body, but it was a whole lot more: I knew instinctively this was the man I was going to marry.

"Up in the room, he opened the mini-bar and poured champagne, maneuvering to take his clothes off at the same time.

" 'Do you have a condom?' I asked.

" 'No,' he replied, his mood shifting to concern, 'but it's okay. I told you I've just been with two women in the past year and I'm sure they didn't have anything.'

"I wanted to go to bed with this man desperately. I *knew* his family, I *knew* his lifestyle. The odds of my getting anything from him were remote. But . . .

" 'But—'

" 'I *should* have a condom with me,' he interrupted, holding me in his arms, 'but if I had one, you'd think I'd been planning to put a move on you, wouldn't you?'

" 'Maybe I should carry one in my purse. But what would you think of a woman who did that?'

" 'Probably that she was—' He stopped short, frowning. 'Oh, I don't know what I'd think. But I guess if every woman carried one there wouldn't be any stigma attached to it, would there?'

"The mood was broken. I should never have said anything. I was flying out to Little Rock the next day, and who knew when we'd ever get together again. I was upset and angry.

"Paul went into the bathroom and I heard him talking on the phone. I was unnerved. Who was he calling? An old girlfriend? He was being incredibly insensitive. What was it he didn't want me to hear?

" 'The phone was staring at me in the bathroom and I thought we could use some more champagne,' he said, returning to the room, 'so I called room service.'

"I couldn't read his mood. He wasn't smiling, but he didn't look too annoyed, either. I wanted to get out of there and back to my own hotel.

" 'I'm trying to be as up-front as I can,' I said, 'and I feel uncomfortable being here. I think it's best if I leave.'

" 'No,' he said. 'I don't want the evening to be ruined. Let's wait to have one more drink and then I'll walk you downstairs.'

"It's over, I said to myself. He's being a gentleman. He probably never wants to see me again, but he's a nice guy and he's not going to be rude. I wanted to run out of that room, but I wanted to be cool and polite as well.

"We sat there uncomfortably for a long minute and he turned CNN on to hear the news.

"Finally the doorbell rang and room service came in with a silver tray that had champagne and a couple of mints on it.

" 'Put it on the bed,' Tom directed.

"After the waiter left, Tom said, 'Why don't you lie down and I'll pour you a drink.'

"Lie down? What was this guy thinking? I wasn't going to start up anything. He pulled me out of my chair and over to the bed.

" 'Tom—' I said, backing off.

"He was grinning and holding up a mint wrapped in tinfoil.

" 'Maybe this will change your mind.' He grinned again, looking completely adorable.

" 'I don't want chocolates,' I protested. 'I'd better be going—'

" 'This ain't no chocolate.' He came over and put his arms around me. 'It's a Trojan! Beverly Hills Hotel Room Service Deluxe!' "

My friend Alice, now happily married to Tom, told me this story. I pondered her words, I remembered the condom scene from *Frankie and Johnny*, and I pictured all the men and women I'd talked to while researching this book.

It seems to me that the major problem that sex presents in the Nineties is the same as it was in the Eighties when I wrote my first book—communication. I've offered many ideas in these pages to make communication clearer. Now I'd like to propose one last suggestion that I hope will make making love—and communicating—easier.

I believe it is women who should buy condoms. If a man knows a woman has condoms in her medicine chest next to the aspirins, or carries a condom with her the way she carries a lipstick, neither of them has to grapple with the awkwardness of thinking that he's planned to "make a move" or that she is "aggressive" or "promiscuous." The whole issue of condoms becomes a nonissue: The woman has one, gives it to her partner, and he uses it.

Does this let men off the hook? Yes.

Does this give women yet another responsibility? Yes.

But I'm a pragmatist. In an ideal world, both men and women would buy condoms and use them. In that same paragon universe, we would be able to talk openly about sex, AIDS, what we want, what we need. But until then, I believe, making love will be much better—and safer—if everyone knows there is a condom etiquette: A woman supplies the condom and the man unfailingly uses it.

Yes, the responsibility is ours, but in accepting this control we are taking control of our health and our bodies. We make the decisions about who our sexual partners are, we take the responsibility for our sexual pleasure, we determine the quality of our relationships with others.

I know this idea will be controversial and politically charged, but I am convinced that lives will be saved if we accept it.

I would like to leave you with this: The number of victims infected with HIV who are women has risen dramatically in the last two years and will continue to escalate unless each of us takes the responsibility to stop its transmission. Experts project that no cure will be found for at least twenty years. The time for safe, healthy sex is now, because AIDS affects all of us. Together we can help to obliterate this devastating disease.

Resources

Information on AIDS

The best resource for up-to-date information about AIDS is:

The Centers for Disease Control and Prevention AIDS Hotline
1-800-342-AIDS
In addition to providing safety recommendations based on the latest research, the CDC Hotline also can refer you to local groups that have information on testing, legal aid, and counseling.

CDC National AIDS Information Clearinghouse
800-458-5231
This unit of the CDC has more detailed medical information and can answer specific questions about HIV, AIDS, and the progression of the disease. They handle requests for bulk orders of pamphlets and other written materials that can be used in workshops, classes, business meetings, or educational gatherings with friends.

Center for Women Policy Studies
National Resource Center on Women and AIDS
2000 P Street NW, Suite 508
Washington, DC 20036
The Center requests that queries be made by mail.

Gay Men's Health Crisis (GMHC) Hotline
212-807-6655
Don't read the name and think it's not for you. GMHC was the first organization to combat the AIDS crisis fiercely and intelligently, pioneering the first AIDS hot line and other ground-breaking services that still serve as a model for AIDS care worldwide. The group serves men, women, and children—heterosexuals and gay men and women alike. They can put you in touch with health and legal counselors, clinics for HIV testing, and provide you with a wealth of the most up-to-date, reliable information on AIDS.

National STD Hotline
800-227-8922
Gives information on all sexually transmitted diseases,
including prevention and safer sex practices. On the
basis of your area code or zip code, they can provide
you with referrals to appropriate clinics in your area.
They can also send you pamphlets on STDs and can
refer you to other hot lines and sources of information.
It may take awhile to get through to an information specialist, but it's toll-free, and the information may help
save your life.

National Women's Health Network
1325 G Street NW
Washington, DC 20005
202-347-1140

Women and AIDS Resource Network (WARN)
30 Third Avenue, Suite 212
Brooklyn, NY 11217
(718) 596-6007

The number to call if you have questions about child
bearing and AIDS is:
Pediatric and Pregnancy AIDS Hotline
(212) 430-3333

To get information on artificial insemination and AIDS,
call:
American Fertility Society
1209 Montgomery Highway
Birmingham, AL 35216
(205) 978-5000

Tests for HIV

There are several tests used to tell if you are carrying the AIDS virus. Most tests look for the antibodies the immune system makes in an attempt to stop the virus from spreading. Others look for the virus itself.

At present, all AIDS tests are carried out on blood samples. But since the virus is found in body fluids other than blood, AIDS tests for urine and saliva are also being investigated. In theory, an at-home AIDS test could eventually be available, much like an at-home pregnancy test. But the authorities are worried about the accuracy of such tests (both false positives and false negatives are common) and the psychological effects of getting test results without proper support and counseling.

Remember, it can take up to six months for the immune system to recognize the presence of HIV and start making antibodies; if you think you are at risk for AIDS, it's important to get tested more than once—after at least six months of staying risk free. Whenever an initial AIDS test comes up positive, a second test is always performed. If that too comes up positive, a third confirmatory test is run, using a more sensitive technique. (This test is also more expensive, which is why it is not used initially.) A person is not considered HIV positive until all three tests have come back with a positive response.

The following lists the basic tests now in use or in development and some of their advantages and disadvantages:

Tests	Advantages	Disadvantages
ENZYME-LINKED ASSAYS (ELISAs): HIV-1 HIV-2 HIV-1/HIV-2	Highly sensitive, detect any trace of antibody reactive to specific HIV strain. Used as initial screening procedure. *Note:* The HIV-2 and HIV-1/HIV-2 ELISA are not yet in common use outside of blood centers. Request them specifically.	Only useful when antibodies are already formed. Results can take up to a week, and the tests can incorrectly identify antibodies that are similar to those for HIV as HIV. Confirmation test required.
MUREX-SUDS TEST *(10-minute test)*	Quick version of ELISA. Requires smaller blood sample. Can be conducted in a doctor's office or clinic.	Same flaws as ELISA. Positive results must be confirmed with Western Blot.
WESTERN BLOT BLOOD TEST	Uses very specific pieces of HIV's protein "coat" to detect HIV antibodies. Much more specific than ELISA. Used as a confirmation test.	Useless unless antibodies are already formed. Results take a week. Can give equivocal results in the early stages of infection.

....

Tests	Advantages	Disadvantages
POLYMERASE CHAIN REACTION (PCR)	Looks for the DNA of the virus itself. Very specific and accurate. Can detect HIV in very early stages of infection. Good confirmation test for less-than-clear Western Blots.	Very expensive and time consuming. Can take 2 to 3 weeks to get results. Now in use only for research.
URINE TEST (not approved)	For use when getting a blood sample is unsafe or impractical. Detects antibodies.	Like ELISA, high rate of false positives. It's also easy for patients to tamper with samples. Will require confirmation test.
SALIVA TEST (not approved)	Very simple screen for HIV. The test's dip stick will change color when it comes in contact with HIV-positive saliva. Eliminates the need for blood sample in first phase of HIV screening.	No more accurate than ELISA. Will require confirmation test.

Where to Buy Condoms by Mail

Although more and more cities around the country have stores that specialize in condoms, Condomania is still the biggest. They have eight stores (see addresses below) and plans to franchise. They also sell mail order. If you live in an area where condoms are still sold out of dusty drugstores, or if you are simply too embarrassed to buy them in person, you can get both condoms and condom advice from Condomania by calling 213-933-7865 and charging the merchandise on MasterCard, Visa, or American Express.

Condomania stores are located at:

7306 Melrose Ave.
Los Angeles, CA 90046

3066 Grand Ave.
Coconut Grove, FL 33133

7021 Hollywood Blvd.
Hollywood, CA 90028

541 Castro St.
San Francisco, CA 94114

351 Bleecker St.
New York, NY 10014

1969 Union St.
San Francisco, CA 94123

758 Washington Ave.
Miami Beach, FL 33139

3049 Las Vegas Blvd. So.
Las Vegas, NV 89109

In addition, you can order condoms from the following companies:

Preventive Products Incorporated
P.O. Box K-270
Brookfield, MA 01506
Founded by a nurse who "was tired of seeing young people die when they didn't have to," this small innovative company offers three very economical condom sampler packs—called Lover Cover Samplers—containing up to

24 different condoms, various lubricants, and detailed instructions on their proper use. Write for details and prices.

The Rubber Tree
4426 Burke Ave. North
Seattle, WA 98103
206-633-4750
This nonprofit organization, run by volunteers of the Seattle branch of Zero Population Growth (ZPG), offers some 65 types of condoms (no novelties) and a host of lubricants, spermicides, dentals dams, latex gloves, books, massage oils, etc. Mail-order sample packs are available. For a free catalog, send a self-addressed stamped envelope.

Many Planned Parenthood centers and AIDS activist groups like GMHC provide free condoms—and information on how to use them. Check your phone book for local listings.

Books of Interest

Comfort, Alex. *The New Joy of Sex*, Crown Publishers, New York, 1991.

Eichel, Edward, and Philip Nobile. *The Perfect Fit: How to Achieve Mutual Fulfillment and Monogamous Passion Through the New Intercourse*, Donald I. Fine, Inc., New York, 1992.

Garrison, Omar. *Tantra: The Yoga of Sex*, Harmony Books, New York, 1983.

Hartman, William, and Marilyn Fithian. *Any Man Can: The Multiple Orgasmic Technique for Every Loving Man*, St. Martin's Press, New York, 1984.

Institute for Advanced Study of Human Sexuality. *The Complete Guide to Safer Sex*, Barricade Books, N.J., 1992.

Johnson, Earvin "Magic." *What You Can Do to Avoid AIDS*, Times Books, New York, 1992.

Ladas, Alice K., Beverly Whipple, and John Perry. *The G Spot*, Holt, Reinhart & Winston, New York, 1982.

Levy, Howard S., and Akira Ishihara. *The Tao of Sex*, Integral Publishing, Lower Lake, Ca., 1989.

Pesmen, Curtis. *What She Wants: A Man's Guide to Women*, Ballantine Books, New York, 1992.

Purvis, Dr. Kenneth. *The Male Sexual Machine*, St. Martin's Press, New York, 1992.

Richardson, Diane. *Women & AIDS*, Routledge, Chapman & Hall, Inc., New York, 1989.

Saraswati, Sunyata, and Bodhi Avinasha. *Jewel in the Lotus: The Sexual Path to Higher Consciousness*, The Kriya Jyoti Zantra Society, Sedona, Ar.

Solomon, Robert C. *About Love: Reinventing Romance for Our Times*, Touchstone Books, New York, 1989.

Stoppard, Dr. Miriam. *The Magic of Sex*, Dorling Kindersley Ltd., London, 1991.